MVFOL

CABBAGEHEAD

HELEN LAROE

Amazon Books

© 2020 Helen LaRoe All Rights Reserved

© 2021 Emma LaRoe Original Cover Art All Rights Reserved

ISBN: 979-8-9858785-7-8

Media Contact:
Email: PR@CabbageheadBook.com

Dear Reader,

This is my story. A slice of my life. It's not meant to bring anyone any more pain. I'm not an expert on the East Area Rapist or Joseph DeAngelo's crimes. I am not an armchair sleuth and following true crimes is not a hobby of mine. In fact, I've never written a book until now. All I know is what happened to me, and I want to share my story with you.

———————————

This book is a memoir. It reflects the author's present recollections of experiences over time. Some names, characteristics, and places have been changed. Some events have been compressed, and some dialogue has been recreated. Opinions and views in this book solely belong to this author and not to anyone who has endorsed it or worked in the production of this book.

CONTENTS

PART 1
GROWING UP

PART 2
MIRYOKUTEKI DA
(THE CHARMER)

PART 3
A BLIND EYE

PART 4
PIECES TO THE PUZZLE

DEDICATION

This book is dedicated to the survivors of the world. Those who have survived mental or physical abuse, rape, narcissists, and bad choices. You are brave and courageous and not alone. Once you genuinely believe this, you will realize that you don't have to survive it anymore. You can walk away from the pain and embrace inner peace. It's right there waiting for you…

ACKNOWLEDGMENTS

The experience of writing a book is both internally challenging and rewarding. I couldn't have completed it without the following people:

A huge thank you to Annie Preston who edited the final draft of Cabbagehead. She was a delight to work with, professional, meticulous, highly skilled, friendly, and honest. Annie's amiable personality made it easy to work with her. I feel I have gained a new friend.

I cannot begin to express my deepest thanks to Shannon Morrison for her editing, encouragement, humor, and moral support while I was writing Cabbagehead. Shannon helped to pull out so many hidden feelings with absolutely no judgment. I will always treasure the time we shared together. It has strengthened our friendship and brought us closer than imaginable.

I would like to thank my niece, Emma LaRoe, cover artist extraordinaire. Emma's talent has always impressed me, and I am so proud and honored she chose to be a part of the production of this book. She is an amazing artist and even more of an amazing person.

A very special thanks to Doug Turner and his late wife, Vicki Marsh Turner. I am grateful for Doug's insight, encouragement, and editing the first draft of Cabbagehead. Vicki's encouragement, enthusiasm, and friendship will remain with me forever.

My deepest gratitude is to my best friend and husband of thirty years, Rob. His love, encouragement, and empathy brought me to the finish line of writing this book. His endless support never wavered, even after dragging him through every chapter a hundred times and wading through a hundred tears.

PREFACE

What the hell did I do?

I married a rapist. He didn't look like one, but then, what does one look like? The one I met had big blue eyes and soft full lips. His entire face smiled, and his eyes sparkled when I laughed at his hilarious stories. I was dangerously attracted to him, like a moth to a candle.

No, the fact he was a rapist wasn't detectable at all. He wasn't a shifty- eyed creep. He lived right under my roof. He slept in my bed. With me. He was my first husband and he lived in plain sight.

He had once shared with me what I believed was his darkest secret about his time in Japan. He seemed remorseful and I trusted him when he said he would never do it again. I was young and he had rescued me from the clutches of another evil. So, I kept his ugly secret buried deep in my head and heart for forty-two years. But it reared its ugly head again to open my eyes to an even bigger secret.

In 2016, the FBI launched a national campaign to identify the East Area Rapist/Golden State Killer. The East Area Rapist wandered the streets of Sacramento, California between 1976 and 1979 stalking, then raping over fifty women. And he got away with it for over 40 years. The FBI wanted the public to consider the following: He would be between 60 to 75 years old, stand about 5 ft. 10 in. tall, have an athletic build, be experienced with military or law enforcement, and proficient in firearms. The FBI wrote, "People who know the subject may not believe him capable of such crimes. He may not have exhibited violent tendencies or have a criminal history."

The FBI chose three composite images to use in their campaign to catch the guy. I looked at the composites and in one I saw a familiar face staring back at me. I thought to myself, *Oh no, Yogi. What have you done?* When you know something is true, but you don't want to believe it, you try to ignore it. You try to forget. You pretend it couldn't be true and even try to prove yourself wrong. But it creeps back into your mind. It haunts you until you do something about it. I dove in. The more details I read about each one of the cases, the more I realized I held many of the missing puzzle pieces. Pieces that belonged to horrific crimes. The crimes and their details shocked me. Learning of each attack for the first time felt like a new stab wound and I grieved for each survivor.

I contacted the FBI and local law enforcement several times. No one was interested enough to listen to the story I needed to tell. I felt silenced and the strong need to speak the truth to help find closure for the women who looked into the eyes of a bright blue-eyed attacker. All of this led me to write *Cabbagehead.*

On June 29, 2020, Joseph DeAngelo, a former police officer, pleaded guilty to 13 counts of first-degree murder and 13 counts of kidnapping. In exchange for 11 consecutive life sentences, instead of the death penalty, he agreed to admit to committing all the other crimes. They couldn't charge him for the crimes of rape and burglary because the statute of limitations had passed. It was part of the deal for him to "admit" to all the rapes. The District Attorney bundled the Visalia Ransacker, the East Area Rapist, and the Golden State Killer crimes and closed them all in one fell swoop. Their goal was to bring closure for the victims and get the files closed. This is understandable, as the cases sat undisturbed for decades, except for a single cold case unit that kept digging for answers and finally got one.

There is glaring evidence supporting the fact two rapists committed the East Area Rapist (EAR) crimes. Physical descriptions don't lie. Witnesses and victims described differences in the build, height, weight, eye color, color of arm and leg hair, and even penis sizes.

The evidence is clear that the EAR was not one, but two monsters who roamed free for over forty years until law enforcement linked Joseph DeAngelo's DNA to some crime scenes committed outside of the Sacramento area. He is the attacker who was captured.

But they were only half right. There was another blue-eyed monster who was horrific in his own right. He was the man I married, the father of my son. He is the man I believe bears responsibility, along with Joseph DeAngelo, for the rapes committed by the East Area Rapist.

Journey with me into my past as I share with you a bit of my younger years growing up and later how I became entangled with a serial rapist.

A MILLION BUCKS 1985

HIS HANDS RAN LIGHTLY OVER MY SMOOTH NAKED HIP, CLUTCHING THE skin on my thigh. He woke me from a deep sleep. My head remained foggy while my eyes opened like two small flashlights needing new batteries. They worked well enough to illuminate Yogi's silhouette. He fondled every inch of me. It was all I ever wanted. It seemed every part of my body was important enough to caress, gently at first and then with urgency. It was how I always envisioned lovemaking to be. Like a blind man searching for just the right freckle on my body.

We moved together in slow motion, savoring every electrical jolt. The smothering of his love enveloped all of my being. It was unfamiliar territory for me. Things with Yogi finally turned a corner. I thought this must be love. It used to be just sex and sex games. That night it was different, more intense with every touch.

Earlier that evening, my friend had a fight with her teenage daughter. It was a big enough quarrel for the teen to want to stay the night with us. She brought her friend along with her who lived in an apartment down the street. Our living room would be their bedroom for the night. Raising teenagers wasn't easy for a single parent, so we didn't mind helping out when we could.

It was Yogi's night off. As usual, he stayed up late either watching T.V. or meandering around the neighborhood. He engaged in his beer drinking marathon, as always.

"Goodnight, everyone. I'm going to bed. See you all in the morning." I had called out to the girls while walking in the direction of our bedroom.

Yogi hadn't followed me, but I figured he wouldn't be long. My eyelids were heavy, and I fell asleep as soon as my head hit the pillow.

The next morning, I felt like a million bucks. I slid out from under the covers and left our room to let Yogi get some extra sleep. Fearing I would wake the girls, I tiptoed to the bathroom and closed the door without making a sound.

In the living room, a light blanket swirled in a mess on the floor in front of the television. Empty beer cans lay on the coffee table, and Yogi's lightweight green shirt was draped over the T.V. screen. It was the shirt he wore the night before. The ashtray bulged with cigarette butts, the front door was unlocked, and the girls were gone.

I wanted to be sure the girls returned home safely, so I called my friend. Her daughter answered.

"Hey, you got up early. Everything okay with you and your mom?"

"Yeah Helen, my friend needs to talk to you."

Her friend got on the phone and began to describe what happened to her the night before. As I listened to every word that came through the phone, my stomach burned like molten lava, and my breathing stopped.

"I grabbed a blanket and laid down on the floor," she began. "Yogi stayed up watching T.V. until I fell asleep. But I woke up to him curled up against me, breathing on my neck. He was under the blankets with his hand between my legs. That's all I want to say. It was horrible."

As I stood there on the other end of the phone trying to digest her words, tears poured from my heart.

"Oh, my God! I'm sorry! I'm so sorry, honey. I'm so sorry this happened to you."

Anger bubbled inside me like one of Yogi's shook-up beer cans. I hung up the phone, then slowly and methodically walked to my bedroom.

"Yogi. Yogi. Yogi," I said, slow and angry. But he didn't respond.

"Yogi," I growled from the pit of my stomach. "Wake up, you motherfucker."

He lay still; nothing.

Out of the corner of my eye I caught a glimpse of his much-loved 38-snub-nose revolver laying on our dresser. I picked it up and remember feeling how comfortable it fit in my hand. I aimed the short barrel of the gun at Yogi's face.

"Wake up, so I can blow your brains out, Motherfucker." My words were low, steady, and slow.

PART 1

GROWING UP

LITTLE MEN 1962

IN THE MIDDLE OF THE NIGHT MAMA TOOK MY LITTLE HAND AND made the sign of the cross by touching my forehead, my chest, then shoulder to shoulder. She whispered, "In the name of the Father, and the Son, and the Holy Ghost, Amen."

Mama slept with me in my twin bed every night. This was how she kept me safe from the demons that roamed our house. I never saw them, but she did. She would often scream out into the night and my father would race from their bedroom to calm her down. She insisted the demons stood in the hallway staring at us while we slept, and they came to take us away. The demons looked like little men. Then Dad would pour her a small glass of brandy.

"Helen, Helen, Helen. It's okay now. They're all gone. Drink the brandy and you'll feel better," my dad told her quietly.

"But they were here. They were staring at us." She tried to convince him.

"I know, I know, but they are all gone now. Shh, you'll wake Little Helen. Lay back down and go to sleep."

If my light was on, they would have seen me pretending to be asleep. My eyes shut so tight my face crumpled. I was only eight years old and tried hard to believe my mama, but every time I looked toward the hallway, I didn't see anyone. Sometimes I would squint just in case those little men noticed me searching for them. Still, no one was there. All I knew was my mama saw them standing there and my dad saw them leave, every single time.

No surprise I wet the bed every now and then. It's one thing for a child to dream up visions of scary things at bedtime, but when your mother wakes to demons, it all must be true. Every night before going to sleep I pleaded with my dad to check under my bed for witches. He always complied and found nothing, which made it easier for me to float off to sleep.

My mother and I shared first names. I suppose it wasn't proper to tack on Junior to a little girl's name, so my dad just called me "Little Helen." Names were important to my dad. When he was born, his parents named him William. After his father died, my father changed his name to his father's name, making himself a junior. He was in his twenties. Mama had a sense of humor. She told my dad she wouldn't call him William or John. She called him, "Jack." The name stuck with him. It's my guess my mama named my older brother, Brian. Maybe she wanted to end the "same name" trend in our family.

Things worsened at home. Mama lit fires in ashtrays and walked around the house, mumbling her incantations to shoo away the demons. She held up the gold crucifix, once attached to her mother's casket, to scare the intruders back to hell. She burned holes in the backyard lawn. Dad had to dig up the burned spots and plant new grass too many times.

Somehow, I knew my life didn't mirror my friends' lives. My friends came home from school, told their moms about their day, grabbed a snack, and did their homework. I came home to a loving mother who fought demons all day long.

When it seemed my mother was losing the fight and the demons were winning, my father got a court order to have her hospitalized.

Walking home from school that afternoon, I tried to get there without stepping on any sidewalk cracks. You know the old saying, "Step on a crack, and you'll break your mother's back." I figured my mom had enough trouble as it was. I made it all the way home without stepping on a single one. That didn't seem to stop the pain ahead for Mama.

Our car was in the driveway, so that meant my dad was home early.

"I'm home, Mama!" I yelled as I slammed the front door and tossed my papers on the sofa.

"There's my Little Helen. Come sit with me," my dad said as he patted his lap a few times.

My dad's face confused me. He was smiling, but it wasn't a genuine smile. His eyes were red, and he looked tired. I gathered something was wrong as I climbed onto his lap. I didn't want to look at his face anymore. As he fumbled for the right words, my little fingers pulled at the yarn loops in my sweater as my right heel swung into the wooden chair.

"Little Helen, you know Mama hasn't been feeling well for a long time, so I took her to the hospital. She'll be there a while, but when she comes home, she will be all better. Mrs. Foster will watch you before and after school until I get home from work."

The neighborhood ladies had something to gossip about now. They all gossiped about my mom from one side of their mouth and spoke sweetly to my father on the other side.

The next morning, I stayed with Mrs. Foster before school. Already she was on the phone talking to another neighbor about my mama. "Oh my god, Wilma, I saw the whole thing. I was watering my plants when the ambulance pulled up to their house. She wouldn't go on her own. I'm with Little Helen now. Let me call you back."

I couldn't even look at Mrs. Foster. Although I was only eight, I knew two things. One, Mrs. Foster had a big fat mouth; and two, my dad had lied to me about taking my mama to the hospital. I'm sure the scenario my mind created was much worse than what happened. I hoped so, anyway.

In the early sixties, any talk of mental illness was hushed. Ladies would only talk of such things in whispered gossip sessions over cups of coffee, in between cleaning the house and folding laundry. Mental hospitals and psychiatrists believed that electro-shock therapy helped those with severe depression or psychotic behavior. Seventy-five to 120 volts ran through a delicate brain to produce a grand mal seizure. They gave patients medication to relax their bodies to avoid their backs and other bones from breaking during the procedure. A frantic spouse or relative would beg doctors to help their depressed and delusional loved ones. It only took the signature of two convinced doctors to perform this procedure on an unsuspecting patient. Treatment for those suffering from mental health disorders have thankfully come a long way since the 1960s.

It seemed the doctors successfully destroyed the demons in the hospital, but they destroyed some of Mama's memories too. She had to relearn how to use a typewriter and to cook some of her best recipes. After they released her from the hospital, our lives seemed to return to normal. I should say our "new normal."

One evening after her return, the four of us piled onto the sofa in the family room. My parents turned an extra bedroom into a room where we watched T.V. in the evenings together. *Have Gun Will Travel* and *Bonanza* were our favorite television shows. We all looked forward to seeing a new episode from a lengthy list of westerns.

Mom sat in her black pedal pushers reading a book on one side of the brown sofa, while I painted my dad's toenails with clear polish on the opposite side. Dad would look down and smile at his clumpy toenails as if I were the best toenail painter around. My brother, Brian, sprawled himself on the carpet in front of the television. I glanced up at the T.V. screen to see Little Joe riding his horse, Cochise, on the *Bonanza* show. Life was back to normal.

CUPS AND SAUCERS

MAMA GRABBED MY DAD'S SHOTGUN AND HELD IT IN FRONT OF THE window shade. We heard a crashing sound and someone prowling around in the backyard moments before.

"Shhh," Mama whispered. "Lay down on the sofa."

She eyed the shade to see what her silhouette portrayed as if she was playing shadow games with me on the wall. Mama hoped to present a shadow of the rifle ready to shoot the trespasser on the other side of the window. She injected a shell into the chamber for an added scare. That sound can't be mistaken for anything else. After that - friend or foe - they were on their merry little way. We lived in a new neighborhood called Northgate, north of Sacramento. Our property fences had not yet been built.

Mama was a kind and thoughtful person. She was calm, playful, and funny. On the flip side, those scary nights when she turned into Annie Oakley, I was afraid for the trespasser.

My father was a marine biologist for the state of California. He was required to travel often throughout the state. Mama always seemed nervous when Dad was away, so when her shotgun routine repeated itself, it never surprised me.

My mother had another inexpensive security alarm system. She placed one of the kitchen chairs in front of the front door. Then she arranged dishes, cups, and saucers on the chair. If a prowler tried to get in the house through the door, the dishes would come crashing down. It would give her enough time to wake up and prepare to shoot.

Despite the short time I spent with my father, I have unforgettable memories of camping with my family. My dad saved massive amounts of time off and blended his work with his vacation days. Working for the Department of Fish and Game had its perks. We camped for weeks in the summer.

I loved waking up to the sound of birds chirping away at each other. The smell of bacon sizzling in a pan and listening to mom clank her pots around the trunk of our car in the morning was music to my ears. It was better than listening to alarm clocks yelling at us or fighting for the bathroom. We experienced real camping. Sure, we had some luxuries from being seasoned campers, like blow-up mattresses and down sleeping bags, but we still peed on the forest floors and swam in streams to get clean.

Swaddled in Dad's green woolen blanket, swatting the smoke from the campfire, we roasted big marshmallows on long sticks we found. Dad would scrape the bark off with his pocketknife and we would be ready to roast. My marshmallow would always turn into a bubbly black mess or fall into the fire. There were times we were all around the campfire, and not a word was uttered. It was as if we needed full concentration to melt the little white pillows over the fire. The sticky sugar covered my brother and me, from the tops of our blonde hair down to the bottoms of our dirty little sneakers.

There is something so special about camping with your family. I can't put my finger on just what it is, but it brings you closer. We needed that closeness after dealing with Mama's illness.

It had been a year since her time in the hospital, and she seemed to be doing much better. It felt like things were finally going well for my family until one afternoon when Mom received a call from Dad.

"I'm having chest pains and trouble breathing," he said; then assured her, "Don't worry, Helen. They're taking me to the hospital to get checked out. I love you. Go ahead with dinner. I will be home soon."

His flight had just landed in Sacramento, returning from a quick business trip. The ambulance had been waiting for him.

Nurses and doctors rushed around the gurney the medics brought in. They all lifted my father onto the operating table. The doctors and nurses worked in unison to keep him alive. They called in the priest assigned to the Catholic hospital that day. He gave my father the last rites, then my dad passed away.

Dad's heart had been in terrible condition. He took medicine for it, but it wasn't enough to keep him alive long enough to see us grow up. Dad was only thirty-nine when he left us. My dad's death devastated all three of us, and we all grieved in our own way for many years.

THE LITTLE HEATHEN

"I HATE ME!" SCREAMED MY OLDER BROTHER AS HE PUNCHED HIS FIST into the bathroom mirror. Hundreds of pieces of glass scattered all over the bathroom. The sound filled the back of the house as the small chards of glass hit the pink ceramic-tiled counter and tumbled to the floor.

Brian wept, but I was too frightened to check on him. My mother hurried to the bathroom and began sweeping the glass away. We did without a mirror for a while. Every time we washed our hands and brushed our teeth, the missing mirror reminded us of Brian's meltdown.

The day before my father died, he had asked my brother to mow the lawns. Brian, like any normal 14-year-old, decided he would rather hang out with friends than mow the lawns. "Yeah, yeah, Dad. I'll mow them when I get back home." My father took pride in our home and landscaping, so he mowed the lawns himself.

Soon after my dad died, my mother told Brian that if he would have mowed the lawns, my father would still be alive. Those disturbing words multiplied Brian's suffering. Mom wasn't thinking when she spouted out such nonsense. She must have been caught in her own anguish of grief to speak such hurtful and wounding words to her son.

Brian was intelligent, but troubled and difficult. Punching the mirror was just the beginning of him trying to deal with his guilt. Dad's death affected him, but there was so much more responsible for the sad life he lived. Brian suffered mental issues since childhood, and soon after my dad died, he began to self-medicate to ease his mental pain.

———

IT HAD BEEN TEN YEARS SINCE MAMA VISITED RELATIVES in Philadelphia. The next summer she booked a flight for the three of us. My mother made me promise that if anyone asked me if they had baptized me Catholic, I would say, "Yes." She recounted to me the story of my first visit to our staunch Catholic Lithuanian family ten years earlier. Happy and hungry, the family sat at the dining table, lavishly decorated and full of delicious Lithuanian food. Everyone gazed upon the beautiful, red-haired six-month-old baby girl: me.

"There's no denying she's Irish with all her red hair."

"No, no, no, that's her Lithuanian blood showing."

"She will bring brightness to every season."

Grandfather had looked down the table at my mother. "I haven't seen anything about her baptism."

"Well, that's because a baptism hasn't taken place," my mother replied. I'm not sure what made her tell the truth that time. Maybe lying to her father in person was too difficult, or she got fed up with being untruthful just to make everyone around her happy.

Suddenly, all our relatives stood up screaming and lashed out at my mother. As they all threw verbal daggers at one another, someone shouted out, "Get that little heathen out of our house!"

Brian ducked under the table and cried while plates of food flew across the dining room. At five years old, my brother remembered it all. One minute they all admired the sweet red-haired Lithuanian baby. Then they all threw the baby out with the bath water. My mother grabbed Brian and me, and we returned to California on the next flight.

Mom, being a bit of a rebel, never had me baptized. I was okay with that. She left that for me to decide myself. And after hearing that story, I never did.

Thankfully, the next trip had far less complications and no one asked the dreaded question. Mom and I were spared all the lying we were prepared to do, and we all had an enjoyable time.

We returned home to find every drawer in the house pulled out and emptied onto the floor. Burglars turned our house inside out. They scattered our clothing about, pulled our mattresses off the beds, and every box in the garage had been ripped open. The inside of our house looked like a yard sale. Mama cried.

It took us days to put everything back where it belonged. Once things were cleaned up, we figured out what was stolen. Brian's friends revealed to him that his weed dealer was the culprit. Along with smoking weed, Brian would sniff glue and other chemicals to get high. With his undesirable behavior, Brian collected a few undesirable friends. Trouble was, we all had to pay for it.

PRISONERS

THE DAY THE POLICE REMOVED BRIAN FROM THE MAPLE WOOD CABINET under the stove was the last time the three of us lived together. That morning my mother called home to see if everything was okay at the house. She drove past six police cars congregating on the corner down the road from our home on her way to work. She knew it had something to do with Brian.

When I told my brother the police were on their way, he began removing all the pots and pans from the cabinet and placed them in the sink. He opened several brown grocery bags, crawled in the cabinet, and ordered me to open the bags and put them in front of him, so the police wouldn't see him. He growled at me, "I will beat the shit out of you if you tell anyone where I am." He demanded I wash the pans.

A few minutes later, the police burst into the house with my mother. They darted from room to room, checking closets and under beds. One officer asked me if Brian was in the house. I shook my head and answered, "No," then continued washing the pans. Another police officer came toward me, rested his elbow on the counter, looked me in the eye and ever so gently asked if Brian was in the house. With hesitation I nodded yes. All I envisioned was Brian's wrath and already felt his fist punching my stomach. I didn't want Brian to know I confessed to the police since I knew he was listening to every word I was saying. I pointed my index finger toward the cabinet several times as if I tapped the air.

The police all glanced at each other. With a soothing voice, the police officer coaxed Brian out of the ominous cabinet. He said, "Brian, we will not hurt you. Everything will be all right. I will open the cabinet door and help you out." It all happened as the officer promised.

They brought Brian to the California Youth Authority. He stayed there for a brief time, then they transferred him to Dewitt State Hospital in Auburn for the mentally ill. They diagnosed him as a "paranoid schizophrenic."

With Brian gone, Mama and I relaxed as our fears died down. Brian's moods resembled a towering seesaw. The highs soared, and the lows crashed. If things didn't go exactly right, he turned angry and violent. Alone, locked in my room became my only refuge when Brian's fury let loose. It meant there would be a hole in the wall instead of a punch in my stomach.

Mama received the same treatment from time to time. She feared him as much as I did. He manipulated her into getting anything he wanted from the best stereo to the newest fastest car. Mama and I re-mained his prisoners when he lived at home.

While at Dewitt Hospital, Mama visited Brian as much as she could and brought him multiple shopping bags filled with candy to share with others in his ward. I imagine she apologized for her comment to him for years after my father's death, thinking everything about Brian was her fault. Every time I visited Brian; my fear returned. Still, I went to make my mom happy. He stared into space so you would have to repeat yourself several times. They medicated him to keep him under control. He had become their prisoner.

I searched for a way to forgive him, but it didn't come until years later when I was more mature and understood his illness and suffering.

THE AIR STOOD STILL 1967

PEEKING OUT FROM UNDER MY COVERS, I SAW MY MOTHER WAS STILL asleep. If we both overslept, it would be nice to stay home together, I thought. She worked for the Department of Gas & Oil as a secretary. I glanced at the alarm clock because it was time for it to make that dreadful sound it did every morning. It didn't go off. I closed my eyes and fell back to sleep.

A few hours later, my blurry eyes opened to a silent room again. I noticed our cat sitting on my mother's stomach. Her stomach didn't change its shape. My mother had not moved since I last glanced at her a few hours earlier. I stared at her a long while until fear motivated me to get up and walk to her bed. Her beautiful hazel eyes, open and glossy, remained still. The color of her skin looked gray and peculiar. I put my left index finger up to her nose to see if I could feel her breath. My heart sank when the air stood still.

I rushed to the kitchen to dial the yellow rotary phone on the wall; I stopped and inhaled much needed air. I put my finger in the zero for the first time in my life, swirled it around, and let it go. The operator answered, and I blurted out, "My mama died in her bed last night!"

I was twelve years old when my mother died. There she lay: cold, rigid, and ashen gray. I had slept 3 feet away from her as she took her last breath. She died directly across from me in a twin bed.

The minutes seemed to crawl by as I was kept on the phone in a one-way conversation. Soon a crew of firefighters blasted through the front door and down the short hallway to my mother's bedroom. I stayed in the kitchen and listened to all the commotion. It turned quiet again. The tall, burly fire chief walked into the kitchen to call a relative for me. Everything happened in slow motion, like a 45-rpm record played at 16-rpm. It became too difficult to comprehend. "Little Lulu" and "Monkeyshines" are nicknames I would never hear my mother call me again.

Without even looking, I reached my hand in the first drawer of the credenza and pulled out the blue address book. I flipped through the worn pages and stopped at my Aunt Ruby's name. I pointed to her name and gave the book to the chief. He called my aunt and introduced himself. He didn't say, "Something awful has happened, and you need to come get your niece." The fact that the fire chief was calling was enough to tip her off to what happened.

The kind fire chief walked me to my friend's house around the corner. There, I waited in shock for Aunt Ruby while the other firefighters removed my mother's body from our home.

Forty-five minutes later Aunt Ruby arrived. She met me with a counterfeit hug. "I'm sorry about your mother." She was always so formal. As tears blurred my vision, I could not form any words to make a sentence. We walked back to my house in disbelief of it all. My aunt and uncle combed through the house looking for valuables. They searched through drawers and cabinets, Aunt Ruby even checked the backsides of all the plates Mama collected, while my uncle loaded up the stacks of items she pointed to.

One of my mother's friends dropped by. "Oh, Ruby, I sure could use this. Is it okay if I take this? Oh, I know Helen would want me to have her jewelry. This is just terrible, Little Helen. Oh, your mama loved you. I need a new hair dryer. Okay to take?"

It was then I realized how much I was alone.

TRINKETS AND THINGS

MY AUNT AND UNCLE FINISHED LOADING THEIR
GREEN STATION WAGON with all the household items they
thought someone might want to steal from my house, and we drove
off. I looked back one last time, to take a mental picture of my home,
just in case I never saw it again.

"Little Helen, why don't you take a nice warm bath. It will help
you sleep better. You can use my fancy bubbles," Aunt Ruby said. She
handed my uncle a pile of sheets and blankets without saying a word. He
knew what she wanted him to do. My uncle pulled out the trundle bed
in my seven-year-old cousin's bedroom and just like that, he inherited
a roommate.

When Aunt Ruby walked by, a trail of expensive perfume lingered.
It made me want to follow her around, only for that reason. Her scent
came from the exquisite tiny bottles she kept on a mirror on top of her
bedroom dresser.

Irish leprechauns must have sprinkled a million freckles on her
polished face and petite body. She walked, moving nothing but her
legs, very rigid and purposeful. Her laugh came from her throat while
her lips remained still without a smile. She seemed to know everything
about everything. She acted shocked if you didn't know what she knew,

even if you were only twelve years old. Despite her arrogant personality, everyone wanted to be her friend and tried to imitate her.

My gentle uncle with his curly ginger hair and smooth, deep voice lived for Aunt Ruby. He remained at her beck and call when he wasn't representing some criminal in the next town. She was Yin, and he was Yang. For the next few years, anyway.

My uncle got a few people together and drove back to my home to pick up the rest of my things. He returned with a truckload and a disappointed look on his face. He described the inside of my house. "It's like vultures broke into a grieving family's home, picked through it, and left it like a carcass of a dead animal. It's just disgusting, Ruby." Then he turned to me. "I'm so sorry, Little Helen," as he went on about the vultures cutting the carpeting out and taking it with them. He was still able to get some of my furniture and personal things out.

Not long after, I noticed my family's furniture and decor displayed in the homes of my Aunt Ruby's friends. She saw my family things as just that, things. I imagined how her friend hoped the coffee table would look fabulous with her sofa. But that was the table where I did my homework each night, Mama looking over my work. I remembered the plate of homemade cookies she put on that table as we watched the *Wizard of Oz* together. Dad had propped up his feet right there, while we had ice cream and talked in silly voices with each other. That table held my family's memories. Now, it had a few artsy magazines on it. I wished I hadn't seen it.

———

AUNT RUBY ALWAYS PLANNED INTERESTING things for my cousin and me to do on weekends. We visited art galleries, science museums, went crabbing in the bay area, camping, and everything else one might dream up to keep a grieving, heartbroken girl from being homesick. They tried everything and nothing worked. They tried in all the wrong places. I needed sincere hugs and to hear, "Everything will be okay. We love you and you are safe with us." But I didn't, and I don't blame them. They didn't sign up to take care of their twelve-year-old niece. They had their own marital problems that were never ironed out.

Nothing filled the void. My mother's death certificate read, "Unknown Cause of Death." How come a coroner didn't find the reason why a forty-two-year-old woman died in her sleep? Mom and Dad were the only things on my mind. My schoolwork took a nosedive. Sadness poisoned my spirit and smiling became just a memory.

Christmas was near. "A drive to San Francisco will do us all good. Little Helen, I can't wait for you to see Ghirardelli Square," Aunt Ruby coaxed. In 1893, Domenico Ghirardelli bought an entire city block and built a chocolate factory. The owners sold the factory and in the early 1960s, the new owners created restaurants and specialty shops within the old factory. The shops were fun to peruse, but I will always remember the chocolate. Crumbling in my mouth and melting on my tongue was pure bliss. Once I finished it, I craved it even more.

Aunt Ruby shopped for hours. My uncle made several trips back to the car with boxes and bags filled with secret presents. I touched oversized wool fisherman sweaters, slid my fingers over a suede wrap-around skirt, ogled leather boots, stared at Peter Max towels, and let my eyes take in all that a young girl desired. Later I found everything I touched or eyed in San Francisco laid wrapped under Aunt Ruby's Christmas tree. We could have opened our own specialty shop with all the trinkets and things. I appreciated her effort, but I didn't need things to make me happy. I needed a sense of belonging and love.

Aunt Ruby worried something was wrong with me that she wouldn't be able to fix. I was a run-of-the-mill B and C student. A few A's made it to my report card now and then. I was always more of a social butterfly. Aunt Ruby took me to visit a child therapist. The therapist gave me many tests and listened to me for several weeks. She finally gave Aunt Ruby the news. She told my aunt that there was nothing wrong with me and explained that I was grieving my parents' deaths. Who knows how much she paid the therapist to figure that out?

I saved up my weekly allowance to buy a bus ticket to visit friends I left a few months earlier in Sacramento. An hour's bus ride brought me back to a place I loved. My friends picked me up from the bus station downtown and I spent the night with them. I didn't tell anyone when I left. I was certain they wouldn't allow me to go.

That night I slept in the same bed with my friends. There was no room to turn over with the three of us in the bed. It was warm, safe, and familiar, feelings I yearned for since losing my family and friends. Little did I know, it would be the last time I would feel a sense of belonging for a long time to come.

CABBAGEHEAD 1968

AFTER MY ADVENTURE TO SACRAMENTO, MY AUNT STARTED TALKING about private schools. We all knew I didn't belong with them, I didn't belong anywhere, but I had to go somewhere.

We visited a few parochial schools in Palo Alto. Although my parents brought me up Catholic, I had a negative association with the church because of the memories of my mother's illness. When I saw all the crosses, I thought of the little men my mama saw in our hallway. Aunt Ruby chose a non-denominational private boarding school in Southern California.

As my uncle loaded the suitcases into the trunk, Aunt Ruby gushed, "Summerhill Academy will be a wonderful opportunity, Little Helen. Your father wanted you to have an excellent education. He wanted the best for you. There is plenty of money for private school, braces for your teeth, and a great college for you to attend. You are incredibly lucky and won't have to struggle." And off we went.

Our flight from San Francisco to Southern California was only about forty-five minutes. Thoughts about attending a private school made me nervous, but also excited to live and go to school with other kids my age.

There we stood, ready to meet the owners of Summerhill Academy,

Mr. and Mrs. Clarke. Our flight was a few minutes early so Aunt Ruby and I waited near the baggage terminal. I wore my orange and green floral mini-skirt and matching jacket my aunt had sewn for me. One thing I never worried about was trendy clothing. My mom made sure I was always in style. It was important to Aunt Ruby, too. My aunt's eyes seemed to crawl over my entire body as she decided whether the clothes that I put together were acceptable. It was the sixties, so I tried to dress modish. I stood a short, thirteen-year-old girl, petite, and blonde. I was quiet when nervous but outgoing the rest of the time. I didn't say a word while we waited; Aunt Ruby filled the silence with small talk.

Mr. Clarke soon arrived at the baggage terminal and helped us load our suitcases into the trunk of the Cadillac that Mrs. Clarke drove. The drive to the school seemed endless, filled with conversation about the beautiful weather that day.

Finally, we drove onto the circular driveway, gravel crunching beneath the tires. It seemed inviting and comfortable enough. The older buildings, surrounded by enormous trees and beautiful bushes, stood beckoning this unknown student. The property displayed itself on about four acres. Orange tree groves were all that surrounded us for miles.

Aunt Ruby first spoke to Mr. Clarke while an amicable girl showed me around the school. She had the strangest first name that I wouldn't even try to spell. She emulated beauty. Her skin, smooth and flawless, and untouched by any blemishes. But her beauty seemed to come from within. She radiated sincerity, a sweetness, and looked you straight in the eyes when you spoke. The sweet girl's smile was toothy, and she pushed her eyeglasses toward her large blue-green eyes with her index finger several times. She was special to have a prestigious position helping Mr. Clarke attract new students to the school.

It was my turn with Mr. Clarke while Aunt Ruby looked around. She already decided I would live there before even seeing the place, so I'm not sure why we were going through the motions of checking it out. We brought my luggage with us. Behind the wooden Dutch door stood Mr. Clarke. The top half of the door opened while leaving the bottom half closed. Vice versa, if you pleased. It had a roll-top desk and an antique table and chair. Books, papers, and odd things were strewn all over the place. It smelled musty and had an orange leather sofa for guests to sit. Mr. Clarke smiled like a cobra and invited me to sit on the sofa with him.

Mr. Clarke appeared older than his age. Black-framed glasses hugged his round, pudgy face. His hair appeared wet, even though it wasn't. When he was silent, his thin lips hid his old, yellowed teeth. He buttoned his plaid long-sleeved shirt up to the very top button and a bolo tie hung from his neck. Mr. Clarke's best attribute was his ability to put you at ease through his playfulness. Was it an attribute?

Mr. Clarke made a few jokes to help me feel comfortable. This soon changed when I asked if students could wear shorts. He chuckled and said, "Well, it looks like you're already wearing shorts. This doesn't have much of a hem now, does it?" As he asked this, his middle finger slid between my legs and up my skirt, searching for the hem. His finger darted around between my legs. I pushed his conniving finger out of the way and sat there speechless with my hands on my skirt between my legs. I shoved my survival-shifter into high gear. As Mr. Clarke changed the subject, Aunt Ruby stepped in to announce, "Welcome to your new school!"

Inside, I panicked. I resisted the tears that begged to leave my eyes. My thoughts were racing, and I contemplated blurting out, "Please don't make me stay here! This old man just put his finger under my skirt!" But I didn't. What would happen if I did, and my aunt didn't believe me? Would she bring me back to her house? I lacked the courage to say anything, like most young girls that age. I swallowed the enormous lump in my throat and followed the nice girl to the girls' dormitory to unpack my suitcases.

They assigned me the best room, as they called it, and I shared it with the amiable girl who showed me around. We slept in the only room with two beds. There were two other dorms with four beds in each room. Miss Finch, the housemother, had a private room off one dorm. Everyone learned early on to grace her best side. Miss Finch either liked you very much or didn't like you at all, and she had a direct line to Mr. Clarke. Miss Finch, a single woman in her early thirties, taught P.E., and sat in on Mr. Clarke's one-on-one student meetings. Anytime Mr. Clarke got a notion to hit a student, Miss Finch was there, watching. The housemother stayed at the school 24/7, never taking a day off. She listened to Jimmy Durante's records on the weekends. Every Saturday all the students helped clean the school, dusting the furniture to the song, "Inka Dinka Do" and mopping the floors to the song, "Make Someone Happy."

Every Saturday evening was Dance Night. The girls and boys met in Mr. Clarke's backyard to dance with each other. He ran a speaker to the outside for music. It was Saturday when I arrived, so I looked forward to a fun night dancing. Everyone looked forward to it because it was the only evening the students didn't have to study for three hours. Sunday night we watched one hour of television. We watched only one program, *The Wonderful World of Disney*.

All the girls ran to Mr. Clarke's backyard together. The boys stood lined up in a row, waiting for us. There were short ones, tall ones, older ones, and skinny ones. When the music started, the boys walked toward the girls to ask if they would like to dance. They all walked toward me at once. I begged for a broken leg, but that didn't happen. The boy in front of me got the first dance. It was my first slow dance. Dancing tied my feet in a knot, and I don't believe I took a breath during the three-minute song by Johnny Mathis. The end of Dance Night couldn't come fast enough.

The first morning there, I woke to Miss Finch ringing a chuck wagon dinner bell. This bell woke all of us up every morning and told us when it was dinner time. My sweet roommate and I got dressed, and she told me which chores I had for the week. I made my bed and swept the floor. She dusted and took the trash out. My roommate checked all the girl's chores each morning.

When it came time to leave for breakfast, she got on her hands and knees and wiped her hands across the entire floor. "Can I help you find something?" She didn't say a word. I thought she dropped something small and was desperately searching for it. Her hands never lifted from the floor. They darted under each of our beds. She stood up, stared at both of her hands and grimaced. She walked toward me with her dirty hands and put them in front of my face.

"See this dirt? My hands should be clean after I go over the entire floor every morning. If they are not clean, then you won't be eating breakfast. We call it a 'Bad,'" she said, emphasizing the last word.

"Wow," I said. Where did that sweet angel-faced girl go? She turned into a minion who deserved an academy award. I learned fast that appearances can be deceptive.

———

IT WASN'T A RELIGIOUS SCHOOL, but the Clarkes and many of the students were Christian. Over the five years I was there, it seemed like the school had a revolving door. Most kids only attended for one year. Once their parents became enlightened with peculiar stories of how this school operated, they pulled their children out as soon as possible. Friends would come and friends would go. I say friends, but they weren't really. They were kids placed at a school their parents believed was something else. Whatever the parents perceived at the initial interview with Mr. Clarke, he served up a big helping for them. If smaller classrooms with one-on-one attention is what they dreamed for their young one, then he would talk that up. If they experienced behavior problems, Mr. Clarke mastered handling any problem. Once the check cleared the bank, kids soon figured out how to play the game to survive.

No one trusted anyone. You couldn't. If you did make the mistake of trusting one of the other students with a secret or misdeed, you found out fast how your butt turned black and blue from a thick piece of wood. They denied us food for a meal or sometimes a full day. The entire school would ignore you for weeks at Mr. Clarke's instruction. Mr. Clarke's mood would determine which treatment you received. Certain kids caught more heat than others. I'm not sure why.

Mr. Clarke used several ways to punish students. Next to the swimming pool was a set of steps. I called them the steps to nowhere. There were three concrete steps that led to a flat dirt area having no purpose. At one time, there might have been another building on the vacant dirt area. The steps, however, had a special purpose. If Mr. Clarke sent you to the steps as punishment, you sat there the entire day. Food, water, and protection from the sun were nonexistent as you sat on the steps.

I couldn't help myself from staring at a student coming inside after spending the day on the steps. Bruce's feet just shuffled into the dining room as if he didn't have the energy to lift them. He stood there, waiting in line for dinner. His face resembled a red tomato growing in the blistering sun. It looked like Mr. Clarke won that day. When I looked Bruce straight in the face, my eyes spoke to him. All they said was, "I know." I hoped that helped in some way. When Bruce reached the serving table, Miss Finch waved him forward using her serving spoon. She didn't allow him to pick up a plate. Bruce didn't eat that day.

The small private school used mental and physical abuse to control its twenty-five students. They used food as a reward or punishment.

"Corned beef and cabbage?" Miss Finch asked me. I did everything in my power to keep a pleasant expression on my face.

"No, thank you, I'll just have milk," I replied and sat down at the girl's dinner table. I always gagged at the aroma of cabbage. My mother loved to cook that repulsive vegetable. Mr. Clarke sat at the head of the girls' table staring at the empty spot where my plate should have been.

"No dinner? Just milk?"

"I don't care for cabbage," I answered politely.

He rose from his metal chair wearing a frown on his face. He walked to the serving table, plopped a big helping of the hot, green, cooked cabbage on a dinner plate, and returned to the table. After pulling his chair out, he put the plate full of cabbage on the floor. "Get under the table. You can eat your cabbage like a dog. Get down there and start eating. Your nickname should be *Cabbagehead!*" he blurted out, laughing cruelly at his own joke.

My peers joined him in laughing as I tried desperately to eat the cabbage without vomiting. My head hung over the plate like a dog. All I could do was plug my nose, and gulp down the green leafy vegetable. He grabbed his camera and snapped a picture of me on all fours, leaning over the smelly plate of cabbage. I was too sick to feel any embarrassment. Later, thinking about the ordeal, I shook with anger and humiliation.

When I was by myself later that evening, I looked up the word, "Cabbagehead," in the dictionary and found that it means a fool or stupid person. Years later, I realized "Cabbagehead" would be the perfect nickname for me.

SCREAMING INSIDE

ONE EVENING DURING STUDY HALL, MR. CLARKE GATHERED EVERYONE into the living room. He carried in a large portable screen and set it up in front of us. Excitement filled the room. We all expected we would see a fun movie or slideshow. We all sat waiting for Mr. Clarke to describe what was coming next.

Miss Finch stepped in and sat herself in a folding chair away from the group. It wasn't a good sign. Even through her thick, black-rimmed glasses, you could see her squinting eyes. With her eyebrows cocked like a blade, her face told all. Miss Finch always mimicked Mr. Clarke's moods. If Mr. Clarke had a beef with a student, you can bet Miss Finch had one too.

A slide popped up of two of our male classmates sitting on the front lawn holding hands. Their faces looked like war prisoners, dark and gray from years of abuse. Mr. Clarke sat them next to each other on the front lawn and made them hold hands. He snapped this picture of them to depict them as gay, he had planned an evening of humiliation.

Fifty years ago, this was horrific to a young boy. While shrinking back in our chairs, the room fell quiet. Our eyes glanced up at the screen, then we all looked away. Those that attended the school longer than me knew what came next. Mr. Clarke encouraged us to attack the boys. He egged us on to jump into the conversation and tear them apart, with no mercy.

"These two seem to think chores aren't important. They'd rather lie around on their beds and watch their roommates do all the work," Mr. Clarke snarled as he tapped his fingers on the table, winding up for something.

Each person in a room had a specific chore to do for the week. The chores were dusting, sweeping the floor, cleaning the bathroom, and emptying the trash. The boys did their chores, just not up to the standards of the room checker. They missed a meal because of it. They already paid a price, but Mr. Clarke hadn't finished with them. These boys were on Mr. Clarke's hit list.

"Look at the boyfriends on the screen. Two birds of a feather. Rebecca, what do you think we should do with them?"

"Mr. Clarke, they should do all the chores in the room."

"And what about you, Darren? What should we do with the hand-holders?"

"They shouldn't get breakfast for a week."

"Helen, what about you?"

"I think all of us should dog pile on your ass and beat the crap out of you, once and for all." I wish I had said that, but I was under the same spell of saving myself from harm, so I joined in with the rest of them. I hated myself for that.

"Well, I know what they need," his blistering voice declared. Mr. Clarke raised up with a glare on his red face and looked at the boys.

"Get up," he bellowed.

Both boys meekly rose from their folding chairs, keeping their eyes pinned on Mr. Clarke the entire time. He took a few steps toward the piano and grabbed his favorite weapon, the board. How did that get there? I never saw him bring it in. He must have brought it in earlier when we weren't there. The board's home base was in Mr. Clarke's office in his bookcase.

The boys trembled in unison. They looked like two slender tree branches in a windstorm. What happened next turned my stomach. It's that violent carnival ride you want to jump off, but you can't because it's too dangerous. *Whack, whack, whack,* the board shouted. Again, on the next boy's bottom. Screams flew from each of their mouths. This went on for several minutes. Then he sent them both to bed. And I suppose Mr. Clarke felt whole again.

———

ONE MORNING I RAN AWAY WITH a tiny girl named Francie. She had the best sense of humor and an amazing inner strength. Not only was she intelligent, but she was a little spitfire of a girl. Her brother also attended the school, but he didn't go with us. It shocked Francie and me how easy it was to leave the school premises. We both ran fast and made our way through the orange orchards until we found a beautiful neighborhood lined with flawlessly landscaped homes. Up the long driveway, we walked to knock on the big wooden door. An elegant older woman answered. We asked her if she would please call us a cab. She did, and we waited at the end of her curving driveway.

The yellow cab arrived and drove us to the airport. He assumed we lived at the beautiful home where he picked us up. I'm sure runaways never crossed his mind until we arrived at the airport and didn't have the money to pay him. Francie and I came up with a hundred stories about why we didn't have our purses with us. He threw his hands up and drove off. Francie and I waved and yelled out, "Thank you!"

We found a restaurant nearby where we parked ourselves in a booth for at least two work shifts. We sat and talked all day long, ordering and paying for food with stolen tips from the empty tables. In the late evening, a food server asked us to leave. Two older guys sitting across from us announced we could wait in their van. That offer scared both of us, and we ran across the street to a woman's restroom at a gas station. It didn't take long before police fists knocked at the dirty white restroom door. They brought us into the police department where they questioned us. We explained to the sergeant what we ran away from in significant detail. We thought for sure, help was on the way. They led us to our cells to sleep for the night. Green walls covered in etchings that read, "I was here," and "glad I did it," was the reading for the day. Though the blue striped mattress was naked and dirty, it didn't keep me from hugging it tight and falling asleep.

The next morning Mr. Clarke greeted us at the jail. The Clarkes brought us both back to the school. That evening we all met at his home with all the girls at the school. Francie and I stood while everyone else sat on his furniture. We found out our roommate, Carla, snitched on us after Francie and I took off. We didn't blame her because that is what you did to survive. Our peers fired out questions, pretending to seek clues as to why we ran away. Soon, out came the board and Francie and I "paid" for what we did. He never spanked a kid; he beat them with the board.

Mr. Clarke hit Francie many times as she cried out, "I'm sorry, sorry, sorry!" It was my turn and in retrospect I wished I had screamed and cried like Francie, but I wouldn't give him the satisfaction as he beat me again and again. He had beat me many times and many times he made me watch others being beaten. I clenched my teeth and hated him even more. I only screamed inside.

A TOTAL CRAPSHOOT

FEAR FLOWED THROUGH MY VEINS EACH DAY AS I
STRUGGLED TO PLAY THE game according to Mr. Clarke's rules.
All of us were good kids trying to play this game, win it, and get back
home as soon as possible. In my case, I knew I would never go home.
I didn't have one, so my goal became surviving with the least amount
of pain, mental or physical. The game was definitely a total crapshoot.

Just when you thought you mastered the game, Mr. Clarke would
switch the dice up on you. It was almost time for me to change clothes
for our gym class. Earlier, I asked Mr. Clarke to check a letter I wrote.
He called me to his office, where we both sat on his orange sofa to go
over everything. "Just make these changes and your letter will be fine."

Miss Finch's whistle screeched, signaling the start of our gym class.
Mr. Clarke rose from the sofa, opened the door that led into a hallway
that separated the girl's dormitory and suggested, "You can change right
here." His hand and finger swung, pointing to the spot where he stood.

My eyes grew wide as I dropped my jaw on his red cement floor.
Half a second later I realized my mistake, *Oh no! My face showed what
I was thinking.*

"Just what do you think I was suggesting?" He was furious. "I meant
you can change your letter there."

Please tell me why I would get up to change my letter in a secluded, dark hallway while everyone was outside for gym class? He said what he meant. He paused gym class while Miss Finch witnessed my beating with his beloved board. My hatred grew like a festering blister. I lived in a haunted house with no marked exits.

———

ONE EVENING, WHILE SITTING ON THE SOFA with Mr. Clarke, he started asking me questions about my mother. "How did your mother pass away? Do you think the things you did made your mother sad and disappointed? Do you think some of your behavior might have caused your mother's death?"

What was he getting at? Losing my mother was still raw. Young and naïve, I fell into this grim hole he created for me. I thought, I guess it's possible. Maybe she did die because of me. The coroner didn't figure it out. Maybe she died of a broken heart, and I am to blame. I replayed those sinister questions in my mind for years.

Study Hall was a quiet time in the evening when we would do our assigned homework. It lasted three hours. If you finished early, you read a book until it was over and time to go to bed. The girl's study hall was in the living room, two tables of four, two desks in the hallway and a single desk by the front window of the living room. Study Hall was so quiet, all you heard was breathing, pencils scratching on paper, and pages turning. One evening, before it was dark, I heard Mr. Clarke's wood board cracking on someone's rear end. I heard painful screams and a voice begging, "No, no, no, please." The screams continued to rip through the summer air that evening.

"When is he going to stop?" I wondered. "Who deserved that kind of pain?" My father had spanked me one time and one time only. As I cried, he picked me up, hugged me, and said, "I'm so, so sorry, honey. I love you and I will never do that again." Mr. Clarke was out of control.

Study Hall remained quiet as if nothing happened. Glancing out the window I saw Paul, a classmate, running out of Mr. Clarke's office wearing only his white underwear. I looked away in case I got caught watching. My heart pounded faster and harder. The site of Paul confused me. "Why did Paul run out of the office crying with only his underwear on?" I had trouble returning to my homework. My heart ached for Paul, and I thought to myself, no one deserved that kind of treatment.

The next morning, we all scrambled into the dining room to eat breakfast. Miss Finch served it, as usual. Everyone sat down to eat their cereal and toast. The boys' room checker came racing in and whispered into the house mother's ear. Her mouth dropped open as she shot up and ran out with him. The rest of us continued to eat and chat. We all ate our breakfast, but I bet we all wondered the same thing: *What the hell is going on?*

A few minutes later the school dust flew as trucks with blinking red lights and loud sirens herded in. They had found Paul dead with his face down in his pillow. No one spoke a word about his death. There was no service, no silent moment, no prayer, nothing. The Clarkes ignored the fact that the checker found one of our classmates dead. We all were curious about what happened to Paul, but we were too afraid to ask. Mr. Clarke took advantage of the culture of fear and left the entire school in the dark about what happened to Paul. No one ever spoke of him again. I haven't stopped thinking about him, even fifty years later.

Days after Paul's mysterious death, Mr. Clarke pulled me aside to tell me that there would be a detective stopping by to ask questions. He looked at me and asked, "Paul was happy here, wasn't he?" He wanted me to agree to his slick question. He wanted to plant the idea that Paul was happy. My body resembled an ice sculpture. I stood there frozen, and bit back my words and nodded in agreement. It was all my body allowed me to do. Inside, I screamed, *You beat him that night! He begged*

4 4

you to stop! He ran from you, almost naked. Did you murder him? I hate you more than anything! The investigators never came, and questions were never asked. The fear of this school deepened within me.

———

I SPENT MY SIXTEENTH BIRTHDAY in trouble for something. It was always something petty. It was a look that was wrong, or a gesture, or an incorrect interpretation of something Mr. Clarke said. We all became trained robots to respond the proper way he wanted. But it never remained the same, so just when you learned the correct response, it would change, then you would be wrong again. This was by his design. It became exhausting. The Clarkes, his two children, and I drove to the nearest ice cream parlor for dinner. We always looked forward to the homemade ice cream for dessert, except that night.

Although it was my sixteenth birthday, I had angered him, so I wasn't allowed to order any food. I sat there watching while they ate their juicy hamburgers and slurped their creamy milkshakes, ignoring me. There were question marks in the server's eyes. Happy birthday to me. They did allow me to open my gifts the next day, by myself.

Mr. Clarke read all our mail, and students couldn't receive phone calls. If you got caught listening to secular music, you would pay the price. Visitation was once a month alternating on-campus one month, then off-campus the next for eight hours. I never received one visit in the five years I stayed there. Aunt Ruby divorced my uncle and she and my cousin traveled abroad throughout Europe. I never saw them again. The Clarkes became my legal guardians. Later, I learned Aunt Ruby stole my inheritance and joined a cult in California. But that's another dark story.

My senior year was my turn to check the morning chores. I didn't like it one bit. I watched my roommates sweep and dust-mop the floors.

They worked on their floors for forty-five minutes. Some girls did better than others. Unless we ate off the floors, I didn't see the point of denying food because of a smidgeon of dust. It was difficult to clean an entire floor and not find something on your hands. The girls watched me crawl over the floor with begging eyes. They begged for approval. No one wanted to miss a meal or have Miss Finch or Mr. Clarke find out you got a "Bad."

By the time I reached around the last bit of floor, I wiped my hands on the underside of a girl's bedspread to remove any dirt. I stood up, gazed at my hands for dust and said, "Let's eat."

———

MR. CLARKE CHOSE THE SAME UNIVERSITY FOR ME AS HE DID FOR HIS daughter and son. I attended college for a year. It was the first time in years I didn't have to go over an entire conversation in my head before letting it leave my lips. I could think and speak freely and wouldn't be punished for not playing the game correctly. I couldn't bring myself to return to the Clarkes when the school year was over.

I wrote a letter to Carla, asking if she would save me when college let out for the summer, and I was back with the Clarkes. She went to the Clarke's school, so she understood my desperation and didn't need any explanation. Carla had been the one who told Mr. Clarke when Francie and I ran away. The plan was for Carla to pick me up the next morning after I returned to California. The long flight and jet lag wore me down. I gathered all the courage I had to tell Mr. Clarke the news of my leaving. I fought a rising panic inside me. I could barely get the words out, the words I practiced for months.

Finally, they came. I said the words to my captor. My heart danced a jig. I, little ole me, made a huge decision to change my life and pursue happiness. Mr. Clarke used every sly tactic in his bag of tricks to change my mind. He mentally worked me over all night long. With my head bobbing and my eyes at half mast, I got a second wind when it was almost time for Carla to arrive.

Only one thought snuck in, *What the hell do I do if Carla doesn't show up?*

PART 2

MIRYOKUTEKI DA (THE CHARMER)

NO DO-OVERS 1974

DREAD TWISTED IN MY GUT. THE CLARKE FAMILY WAITED IN MR. Clarke's office for me to come say goodbye. There was no way I was about to walk back to his lair for anything. I feared Mr. Clarke would come out to stop me from leaving.

Never looking back, I rushed toward my friend's car and to my freedom. As I opened the door of that old white car, I decided I would leave behind my tormented spirit on that pebbled driveway in front of the private school.

I climbed in, slammed the door, and yelled to my friend, Carla, "Let's get out of here! Go, go, go!" Carla put the car in reverse, turned, and sped off.

I did it! I broke away from that cage they called a school, just like a phoenix. I was proud of myself for taking that huge step of leaving. I knew it was the right thing to do. I waved goodbye to all my painful memories. Unfortunately, it wasn't that simple and many hid in the baggage I lugged along anyway.

Everything about the school had been wrong and yet leaving it scared me. It was all I knew. I didn't possess confidence, life skills, money, or a plan. All that had to wait. I only had the victory of my escape, relief and comfort, and a pocketbook full of optimism. Even the stale perfume smell from Carla's car was more welcome than all the fresh air I inhaled while surrounded by the fresh orange orchards at the school. I made the right decision.

Carla and I both talked a mile a minute, interrupting each other, squealing, and laughing. It would be a couple of hours from the private school to our new apartment in Oceanside, CA. I glanced down to the left of me and spotted a pack of Carla's cigarettes. *Hmm*, I thought to myself. *Why not?* I lit the cigarette right up and started the terrible habit that chased me for years.

Our drive time went by fast. "Oh, Helen, I met this guy downtown the other day. You are going to love him. He is hilarious and will keep us laughing all day long. He's going to move in with us!" She smiled and chuckled as the words left her lips. Carla always had a nervous chuckle.

"Oh, yeah?" My mind raced with thoughts, worried and fearful thoughts. What the heck was she thinking? Some strange guy she just met was going to live with us? Really? Carla glanced over and noticed the fear in my eyes. She realized that didn't sit well with me.

"Don't worry. My instincts are stellar. His M.O.S. (Military Occupational Specialty) was military police in the Marine Corps. He got discharged about two weeks ago from Iwakuni, Japan. See, so he's kinda like an ex-cop."

"That does make me feel better. But Yogi? What kind of name is that?" I asked.

"It's his nickname. He can help us with the rent," Carla said as she pulled the car into the driveway of the apartment complex.

Carla opened the door to our apartment and watched me race through it, both of us smiling the entire time. Her parents pulled her out of the private school a few years back, but she remembered what I experienced. She lived through it herself. While watching me, Carla got to relive that initial sense of freedom all over again. Almost crying, I blurted out, "I love it!"

The two-bedroom apartment was newer, but only had one bathroom. I could foresee Carla and me sharing it. The living room sofa would be my bed for a while. I didn't mind. I whisked away any negative thought and replaced it with a positive one. Nothing could make me believe I made the wrong decision. The past five years were like balancing on a razor blade. No matter which way I tried to move, I always got cut.

We spent the day putting our things away in the new apartment and catching up with all the private school gossip. I was exhausted, still jet lagged from the day before, not to mention that Mr. Clarke kept me up all night to talk me out of leaving. Carla wanted to grab a bite to eat and go bowling with some friends. "Oh man, I'm so tired, I need toothpicks to keep my eyes propped open."

Carla huffed and poked through her purse. "Here, take one of these. You'll be fine soon."

"Okay," I said as I placed the mysterious pill on my tongue and took a swig of soda to wash it down. "What was that anyway?"

"Oh, a diet pill I take every so often," Carla said as she pushed the bottle of pills toward the bottom of her purse.

"A diet pill? Isn't that speed? What the heck, Carla?"

"God, Helen, trust me. You'll be okay. I won't let anything bad happen to you."

By the time we got to the restaurant, I couldn't eat. All I could do was talk or laugh. Carla ate her hamburger, and she ate mine too. We met her friends at the bowling alley. They weren't what I expected. I suppose I was judgmental, but I remembered Carla from the private school. "Oceanside Carla" and her friends drank, smoked weed, took diet pills, and had sex before marriage. Most of the guys cursed every other word. She had changed so much in the time we were apart, while I had stayed behind, locked in Mr. Clarke's purgatory.

———

CARLA AND I DROVE DOWNTOWN to the pizza parlor where Yogi worked. She spotted him behind the counter tossing green and red peppers on the dough. There he stood, about 5 foot 10 inches, athletic looking, brown hair, and bright blue eyes. He was a 22-year-old ex-military police officer, and he carried himself just like that. Yogi took a break from throwing pizza dough in the air and came out to sit down with us. The three of us talked and Yogi assured me we all would get along fine. Sure enough, Carla was right, I liked Yogi.

When Yogi joined the Marine Corps, they sent him to Parris Island, South Carolina, to complete bootcamp. After graduating, they whisked him off to Iwakuni, Japan, where his MOS was military police. The control and respect that came with the position fed his ego.

That afternoon I learned that while in the service, Yogi received his nickname after the cartoon character, "Yogi Bear." The show debuted in 1958 on the *Huckleberry Hound Show*. William Hanna, Joseph Barbera, and Ed Benedict created it. The show starred "Yogi Bear" and his sidekick, "Boo Boo Bear." The bears lived in Jellystone Park. Yogi Bear's main pastime was stealing picnic baskets from visiting campers and making his own picnic out of their lunches. The bear sometimes spoke in silly voices and rhymes. A well-known phrase of his is, "I'm smarter than the av-er-age bear!" Yogi, the person, used this phrase often when he was clowning around.

While in the Marine Corps, several marines shared one community refrigerator. Yogi would rifle through the refrigerator and eat other people's food without asking. He ignored names on anyone's bags because it meant nothing to him. He took what he wanted. No one had to ask what happened to their last piece of lemon meringue pie or bologna sandwich. They knew who took it. Yogi's peers gave him the nickname, "Yogi" and it stuck with him for decades. When Carla and I called his name, he responded, "That's me, I'm smarter than the average bear."

Yogi had trouble telling the truth. It wasn't easy knowing what happened because he embellished every story. To me, Yogi possessed the ability to use creativity in his storytelling. But with every fault he had, I found an attribute. I saw the positive side of him. Carla had much more experience with funny guys who made you believe you were the prettiest girl, or the best, or whatever you needed to be. She had a realistic outlook because she already experienced guys who were losers and out for two things: money and sex. I had yet to learn those life lessons.

Amazing how an eighteen-year-old virgin would be in such high demand. I understood nothing about sex. My mother never discussed it with me, nor my aunt, nor the private school I attended. I figured out the penis slid into the vagina, but that was about it. I had never seen a penis before.

It seemed everyone I met was aware that I was a virgin. Did Carla tell everyone, or were these predatory fellows that good at figuring it out? Carla's male friends would trip over themselves just to get near me with their, "Hey baby, you sure are looking good." They licked and smacked their lips as if they ate a piece of the Colonel's chicken. They all grossed me out, and I did my best to avoid them.

One night, I approached Carla while she made a salad for us. She told me a story the day before, mentioning a word I didn't understand. It took me time to gain the nerve, but I decided to just ask her.

"Hey Carla, what is cum?"

She kept her head down, still chopping the cucumber. Carla's upper body shaking, she let out a laugh. "Are you serious, Helen?" I gave her an offended look. She described the act of sex, then said, "So, then he cums inside you."

Still confused, I asked, "He comes where? Where does he go?"

Later, when we talked about her good friends who were an interracial couple, a thought popped in my mind.

"So, is James' cum black?" At that point Carla had to drop her paring knife and let out an unrestrained laugh. When she finished laughing, she explained everything. I was an eighteen-year-old girl with less sexual knowledge than a ten-year-old. I just began to experience peer pressure, and it put me back into survival mode. It seemed to be the only mode I was familiar with.

———

ONE EVENING, CARLA INVITED HER PARENTS FOR DINNER. Yogi was working that night, so it would just be the four of us - Carla, her father, stepmother, and me. Carla cooked like a pro. She made homemade spaghetti, Caesar salad, and crunchy bread. New York cheesecake topped off our meal. I tried my hardest not to look at her dad but couldn't get past it. I wanted to stab him in the eye with my salad fork.

At the private school, Carla had confided in me about her father's sexual abuse. He'd abused her for several years after her mother passed away when she was young. Her father remarried and continued his abuse. Carla said her father told her he couldn't help himself because she looked so much like her mother, and he missed her. He didn't seem to know how much pain he caused Carla. Pain that followed her for years. Why did she cook him a meal and exchange small talk all evening? The same reason I stayed and put up with Mr. Clarke's mental and physical abuse for so long. You do it to survive because you either don't have another way out or you are afraid of the way out.

We all stood up to say our goodbyes. Carla's stepmother chatted a minute with her while her dad told me how wonderful it was to see me again. He wrapped his arms around me and kissed me square on the lips. When he removed his wet lips from mine, I stood there stunned.

"Come visit us sometime," he said casually.

"Not on your life," I wished I had said. I stared at him while he rested his arm on his wife's shoulder and walked out the door.

———

YOGI GOT FIRED FROM THE PIZZA PARLOR. It had something to do with his boss. They didn't get along very well. His young male boss ordered him around and he wasn't about to deal with that. At least that is how he told the story. I didn't have a job yet, so there we were, both dependent on Carla. Carla was more upset with Yogi's unemployment than mine. Their relationship turned tense.

I walked into the living room one afternoon to find Carla bent over in pain. She didn't know what caused it. Yogi and I rushed her to the hospital. We waited for hours to hear the outcome. Carla experienced a gallbladder attack. The doctor told her the gallstones were too big to pass. They planned to operate. We didn't have our own cars, so we used Carla's car to drive back and forth to visit her in the hospital. It was a time when they had you stay in the hospital until you were well enough to get around on your own. She stayed in the hospital for a while, then recuperated at her parents' home. Carla's parents invited me to stay with them, but I turned down their offer. Over my dead body.

James and his girlfriend, Donna, stopped by to visit Yogi and me. The refrigerator only held lunchmeat, tortillas, and condiments. Yogi had his weed, so to him, life was good. They invited us to go to the drive-in movies. We all went to watch *The Exorcist*. James had waited for the movie to hit the drive-ins. He and Donna sat in the front seat while Yogi and I sat in the back. Yogi inched his way closer and closer to me, sliding his arm around me. Donna kept turning around and smiling at us. She was curious if we were making out. I squealed at the scary parts, and each time Yogi drew me closer to him. When the movie ended, James drove us back to the apartment. My hands fumbled around my purse until I found the key to our place. We both turned around at the same time to wave goodbye to them.

Once inside, we both roamed around the apartment for a few minutes, doing unnecessary things. I sat down on our purple sofa, put my feet up on the white French provincial table and looked at him. I contemplated losing my virginity. Carla and her friends claimed I was overdue in losing it. I was a weirdo, a full-fledged weirdo. If I stayed a virgin, I might as well have sat at a private school listening to Jimmy Durante's records, employed as a housemother. That image was a nightmare. I wanted to fit into a normal world and be an actual person. Yogi had played it cool and was winning me over by being nice, charming, and funny. Right then, I made the major decision: It would be Yogi. I had an idea it would happen that night, anyway.

As if he could read my mind, Yogi walked silently across the floor and reached out for my hand. I stood up, and he led me to the bedroom. He removed his clothes then, while trembling, removed mine. In a high pitch he squealed, "Damn!" as my breasts tumbled out of my bra. His full lips enveloped mine, while he softly placed me down on the bed.

I prepared myself to scream when he entered me, but it didn't hurt like Carla described it would. It was over in a minute.

The first thought that crept in was, "So, that was it? All the hype, and that was it?" I'd had the notion it would last much longer than it did. (An orgasm? What the hell was that?)

When I sat up, something wet flowed out of me and onto the sheet. *Oh my gosh!* I thought, *Did I just pee on Carla's bed?!* I stood up fast to check. Then I remembered Carla's description of cum, "Oh, so that's cum. Alrighty then," I said aloud.

Yogi jumped up to turn the light on and suggested we go out for coffee. He grinned, "Wear my jean jacket without your bra."

I wore his jean jacket, but it seemed like I swam in it. Wearing Yogi's jacket represented his shout out to the world: *She's mine now!*

It barely seemed like a rite of passage. Technically, I guess I crossed to the other side, but I was left disappointed. I couldn't figure out why. I know now that love had been missing from the entire act. Our first kiss happened while sliding on the bed naked together. We missed the chance to look at each other dreamy-eyed and passionately kiss one another. We missed that wait that leaves you delirious until you can see and kiss that person again. No love letters and no longing to meet again. We really didn't even know each other. There are no do-overs after you lose your virginity.

FREE RIDES

IT WASN'T LONG BEFORE YOGI AND I HAD TO MOVE
OUT OF THE apartment. Neither of us had the income to keep
it going without Carla. Our brilliant idea included hitchhiking to
Sacramento to wait for my inheritance check. The Clarkes needed to
pay me the balance of my inheritance. We left on foot with only Yogi's
paycheck. All my clothes and few possessions sat in my room as we
began our excursion. I still don't know what we were thinking.

We made it to the freeway and stuck our thumbs out. Before that
day, I had never hitchhiked, but I wasn't nervous. Yogi had experience
and street smarts. It took but a minute after our thumbs popped out and
our first ride stopped to pick us up.

The woman stopped several feet ahead of us. We both ran to the pas-
senger door. Yogi opened it and when he did, a couple of cans and some
papers fell out of her car. She didn't seem to care. "Where ya kids headed?"

"We're trying to get as close to Sacramento as we can," Yogi said.

"Well, I'm not going to Sacramento, but I'll take you as far as I can,"
she said in an expressive voice.

She introduced herself as Ruthie. Before we got in, she had to move
all kinds of things around to make room for us. The car was full of
papers, books, bags full of clothes, and brown paper bags full of food.

I could tell Ruthie was lonesome and happy to have picked us up. She wore the biggest pink, floral moo-moo I ever saw and earrings that looked like fruit. Her earrings jangled around when she moved her head while talking. Ruthie was a big lady and might have weighed four hundred pounds or more. Her personality was even bigger.

"Bet you didn't know I was an actress. I acted in a Hollywood movie and played the fat lady in a circus. Why they gave me that role I will never know," she said, roaring with laughter. She was the perfect driver to sit next to Yogi. They carried on with one another as if it were a talking competition. I sat in the back catching bits of their animated conversation, drifting in and out of consciousness. Both heads moved back and forth, earrings were swinging, and I heard lots of laughter.

We got to Ruthie's destination, and she let us out. Our second driver made me miss Ruthie. I never caught his name, but right off the bat this guy told us he'd just gotten out of prison. I decided against taking any naps in the back seat of his car.

He seemed lonesome, too. He shoved an eight-track tape into the player, listened to a few songs, took it out and pushed another one in, over and over throughout the entire ride. We got to know Johnny Cash and Elvis songs by heart by the time our ride ended.

Despite his nervous behavior, Yogi kept him occupied with colorful stories about his time in the Marine Corps. Every so often I looked over the front seat to peek at the speedometer. Our car passed all the cars on the freeway, but I wasn't about to suggest we slow down. We didn't know why he spent time in prison, but it felt good to reach the ex-convict's destination. He dropped us off at the bus station on 18th and F Streets, in Bakersfield, CA. where we said our goodbyes.

"Man, that guy was speeding, and I don't mean just the car," Yogi said as we walked down the street, figuring out where we were and what to do next.

"Oh, was he taking drugs? I thought he was just a nervous wreck. Glad we got here in one piece." *Now what?*

BIG HEARTED BAKERSFIELD

GHOSTS HAUNT THE SEVENTH FLOOR AT THE PADRE HOTEL, ACCORDING to some Bakersfield residents. The city had condemned the hotel because of a major fire on the 7th floor in the 1950s which killed several hotel guests, including children. In 1952, an earthquake trapped and killed a large group of children in the basement, unable to make it to safety. The hotel experienced more tragedies including several suicides from its roof.

In 1928, the Padre Hotel opened as a luxury hotel and restaurant. When Yogi and I arrived, there was nothing luxurious about it. It was a seedy hotel with an eerie silence when we showed up. On the main floor there was a bar, cafe, and a small barbershop. The bar was full of loud old drunks and barflies.

A frail, long-haired woman who appeared to be in her nineties welcomed us to the hotel. She took our money and whispered our room number. The interior of the hotel was so gloomy; I thought we would need a flashlight to find our room.

It was to be our new home for a while. There was no television or radio. No one came to fluff the pillows or change the sheets. We didn't find little expensive chocolates on our pillows beckoning us to eat them. Our room was bare-bones and in serious need of updating. Despite all it was lacking, it did have a mini refrigerator that kept our Kool-Aid and bologna cold. Those were the only two items of food that ever made it into that refrigerator. We didn't complain a bit. We were simply happy to have a safe place to stay.

Whenever we told people where we lived, we would get strange looks and were often told, "That can't be. They condemned the Padre Hotel years ago. No one can live there now."

Milton Miller bought the hotel in 1954, two years after the earthquake that caused the basement to collapse. The city wanted him to bring everything up to code. He had it out with the city council regularly. They condemned most of the upper floors. I heard others say that Milton Miller could be a little *over the top*. Once, Milton positioned a fake missile and attached it to the hotel roof and pointed it at city hall. Many people we talked to called Milton old and cranky, but we found him to be kind and generous. He allowed us to stay, even when we couldn't come up with all the rent.

We only had one set of clothes each. I washed our clothes in the bathtub with little bars of hotel hand soap. I opened the windows and laid our wet clothes on a chair nearby. Our clothes had to take turns drying by the window. If they didn't dry that night, we wore damp clothes in the morning, which is usually what happened with our jeans. Even in the summer, it was no fun at all.

We would leave the hotel several times a day with no destination in mind. We spent most of our time walking around downtown and mooching cigarettes to smoke. It made no difference what brand someone gave us. Yogi taught me how to tilt my head, use a closed smile and a few slow blinks before asking. With the guy smokers, we got a few more cigarettes this way.

Sometimes we got lucky and found a dropped dime or quarter on the ground or found change left behind in a public telephone. Begging for food and cheating owners out of their rent money turned into our daily lifestyle. Still, my life seemed much better than living at the private school.

We found a diner on one of our walks and sauntered in. It looked like it had seen better days. Everything from top to bottom and in between this diner was covered in a thick patina of age and grease. We sat down at the counter and looked at a menu, pretending we had the money to order *anything* on it.

Yogi pulled the change from his pocket, did a quick count, then ordered one cup of coffee and one order of toast.

The server turned to me and asked, "And what will you have, darlin'?"

I wanted to say, *Everything on the menu!* Instead, the words I reluctantly said were, "We'll just have the toast and coffee, thank you." When the order arrived, we shared the toast and drank coffee from one cup.

It had been a long while since our order was placed. Yogi and I looked at each other with raised eyebrows, nothing but a single crumb and a dry mug in front of us. Our eyes roamed the cafe, wondering where our server had vanished to. We were ready for another cup of hot coffee to fill our still empty bellies. It had been several minutes since we last saw him.

Well, it turned out our server was the owner of the restaurant and a generous one at that. He suddenly reappeared and brought two plates full of scrambled eggs, bacon, crunchy hash browns, fruit, and a side of pancakes.

"Breakfast is on me!" he declared as he placed the masterpieces in front of us.

"Oh my gosh, we appreciate this so much," I practically swooned.

Yogi and I didn't speak another word. Our forks moved in haste as we enjoyed every little scrap of that breakfast. It had been a long while since we had a real meal that included all the food groups.

When we finished, the owner took our plates and asked me if I wanted a job. I squealed with delight and almost cried. It was my first actual job, not counting babysitting or house cleaning. He handed me an apron, an order book and pencil, and set me loose in the town cafe.

The cafe owner took me under his wing and made sure no one there took advantage of me.

I will never forget the time the owner found out that the projectionist from the dirty movie theatre across the street called to order his lunch and have it delivered by me. I had climbed up the rungs of the handmade wooden stairs that led straight up to where the projectionist worked and brought him his lunch. While waiting for him to retrieve his money to pay for the lunch, I looked to my right and witnessed a couple having sex on the screen. When the money hit my hand, I bolted down those stairs and back to the cafe. When the owner asked where I had been, out of breath, I told him what happened. He lunged from behind the counter, metal spatula in hand, wearing his dirty white apron, and flew across the street before I knew it. I never saw the projectionist again.

Sometimes the people of Bakersfield reminded us of the characters from *The Andy Griffith Show*. Any minute, Andy Taylor and Barney Fife were about to come out of the drugstore to tell us to quit bumming cigarettes from the town folk. The good people of Bakersfield took us in, and we fell in love with their city.

ROAMING THE NIGHT

"DON'T YOU DARE, HELEN, DON'T CRY. DON'T YOU DARE CRY," I THREATENED myself in a furious voice. But then a surge of salty, warm tears ran down my cheeks and dripped onto my chest. Tears saturated my purple sweater in all the sadness of thinking Yogi abandoned me and would never come back.

Yogi got a job at a local print shop. It seemed things were looking up. We both left at the same time each morning, but I got back to the hotel first. Every Friday was payday, and every Friday he was several hours late in returning after work.

Not a Friday went by where he didn't come home to find me crying. Each time he waltzed in, reeking of beer and sweat. Thoughts of being alone had terrified me. With this knowledge, I gave him a license to do whatever he pleased without considering me.

Every night before bed, Yogi took a long walk by himself. He told me he needed to smoke a joint and clear his head. He didn't want to smoke in the hotel for fear he might get caught. So, off he roamed in the night, and I would eventually fall asleep alone. He somehow mastered re-entering the hotel room and getting into bed without waking me.

It wasn't more than six weeks before they fired Yogi from his printing job. I can't count how many times employers would fire him in the years to come. He was funny, friendly, and interesting to be around; on the other hand, he just couldn't get along with male superiors in the workplace. He would explode with anger about something and blame it all on them, never accepting responsibility. No one would put up with his behavior for long, and he would be out searching for work again. For the longest time, I believed all those "assholes" really were out to get him.

———

IT WAS TIME TO LEAVE BAKERSFIELD. We walked around the corner of the Padre Hotel, hopped on a bus, and headed back to southern California to pick up my inheritance check. Don't ask me where we got the money for the tickets. We never saved a dime from our paychecks or my tips. Yogi was habitual pot smoker, so I know some of our money went to that. The bus left early so there was no time to say goodbye to my guardian angels. I only knew them for a few months, but I would still go on to wonder if they missed me as much as I missed them.

I slept most of the way to Los Angeles. Yogi kept waking me up to talk. Have you ever heard the saying, "He could talk your ear off"? I should have been earless. Yogi never had a loss for words on any subject. His goals were to either make you laugh or talk you into liking him. He was great at using conversation as a diversion to throw you off thoughts when he wanted you to stop thinking about something. He wanted to control your thoughts about him. The long drive was boring, and I was tired from getting up so early. All I wanted was to close my eyes to prepare myself for how the conversation would go when I met up with one of the Clarkes. I didn't relish the idea of seeing any of them again.

When we finally arrived in Southern California, a college friend met us at the bus depot. I didn't know her that well, but we had kept in touch, and I wanted to see her before we left for good. Mandy was a good person, kind and very trusting. She took us to her house and asked that we wait there a few hours while she worked. Her parents and sister were gone also. Yogi and I both sat in the living room stiff and uncomfortable. We could only imagine Mandy's parents or sister showing up and the long explanation we would be obliged to give them about who we were and what we were doing in their house.

We decided to leave a note and continue on our way. I wrote a letter thanking her for her friendship and picking us up at the bus station. After I used her bathroom, I was ready to go, only Yogi wasn't in the living room anymore. I searched for him through the large, beautiful home and finally found him in Mandy's younger sister's room. There he was, standing in front of her dresser with the first drawer open fondling a pair of her panties. "What are you doing? Let's go. We have no business here," I said like a mother to her child. I shut the drawer and said, "Come on."

We arrived at our destination and picked up my check. The Clarkes' son was the only one to show up. He gave me the check, said goodbye, and left. It played out nice and smooth, without a hitch. The check was for a whopping $1,600. That day marked the last time I would have to engage with the Clarkes for anything. There was nothing more to say to any of them. Sorry, guilty, or sad, did not enter my mind. Realizing what just happened caused my emotions to run wild. It was as if I was held underwater, pulled up, and took that first breath of fresh air. All the years of manipulation, physical and mental abuse, guilt, and punishment for playing the game wrong, seemed to vanish. Seems like I finally rolled a seven. I was over the moon, and it felt good.

We made our way back to Los Angeles, cashed the check, and spent the night at the Hotel Cecil. The entrance to the hotel was stunning and welcoming. Once you made it past the glitzy entrance and check-in counter, it looked like any other old, dark, and dingy hotel. The hotel had been built in 1924 and had 19 floors with 700 rooms. It did well until the Great Depression, then the area went downhill with transients.

The neighborhood was known as Skid Row. Of course, we stayed there; after all, the nightly rates were cheap.

The Hotel Cecil had a grim past. There were more than 13 suicides and countless gruesome murders. Drug dealers, transients, prostitutes, and people with checkered pasts lived at the Hotel Cecil. A few well-known serial killers lived here at one time. Today it is known as, *Stay on Main*, and has been beautifully refurbished to help change its dark past.

Despite a few hurdles, I looked forward to a bright future with Yogi. Happiness overwhelmed me about what would happen next. Yogi wanted to fly to Atlanta, Georgia, to visit one of his Marine Corps buddies, then fly on to Massachusetts, where his family lived. We grabbed a flight out of Los Angeles. On the airplane, we toasted to our new life together. Our plastic cups rubbed together, and we sipped and smiled. I could feel our fairytale was about to begin. Fairytale?

PART 3

A BLIND EYE

THE WARNING

THERE WE STOOD IN THE ENORMOUS CITY OF
ATLANTA, GEORGIA. WE ended up in a part of town where corruption was just a way of life. Here the successful criminals dropped
quarters in the palms of the less fortunate and preyed on any newcomers
that dared to cross their path. It was unfamiliar territory to me, but not
for Yogi. This city was alive and moving. Yogi and I were the newcomers
in town. We faced this hub of lawlessness head on.

We got a room at the Peachtree Hotel. The Padre Hotel was down-
right cozy in comparison to our new humble hotel room. The place was
compact and looked dirty. I couldn't quite ever put my finger on what
made me feel like a thousand spiders crawled the entire floor. Every
time I entered the elevator, a creepy looking man would ask me if I
knew Jerry. A different man each time, but their eyes slowly moved
from my breasts to my crotch, then up to my face. Every single one. I
thought this Jerry guy was a popular fellow at this seedy hotel. Yogi was
out looking for work most of the time, but no one ever asked him on
his elevator rides whether he knew Jerry. Eventually, I found out Jerry
was the hotel pimp.

I learned to navigate Peachtree by myself. It was the biggest, busiest
street I ever saw or crossed by myself. Better pay attention or you could

get mowed down. These cars were in a hurry. There I stood, waiting for the slow light to change. A young Black man was waiting next to me and started a conversation about the weather. He mentioned the sky's beauty and that it had been a splendid day, marked with blue skies, and billowing white clouds. I agreed with a smile. A middle-aged white man crossed in front of us, arranging his frame against the traffic facing both of us. He glared at the friendly Black fellow and then back at me. His facial expression confused me. "Everything okay?" he asked.

Puzzled, I responded, "Yes." The light turned and the three of us walked our separate ways. This scenario would play out several times throughout our stay. Get close to a Black man and you could expect nearby white males to check if you were okay.

Our stop in Atlanta lasted longer than we expected. We planned to fly on to Yogi's home state of Massachusetts. Yogi and his friend, Alan, were both stationed in Iwakuni, Japan together. Alan had been transferred to Albany, GA. Albany was about a three-hour trip from our hotel. He stopped by for a brief visit one afternoon telling us he had to return to the base shortly.

Alan and I sat alone for a few minutes while Yogi walked to the hotel lobby to grab a few sodas. Alan's eyes locked with mine and his facial expression turned serious. He only had time for very few words. "You need to get away from Yogi now! He is no good. I'm serious. You need to go back home. Figure out a way!"

I told Alan, "I don't have a family or a home." Before we could say any more, Yogi returned. Alan had driven those three hours to meet me and deliver the warning. A warning I had no idea how to face.

CUNNING REMORSE

I WAITED UNTIL ALAN WAS LONG GONE BEFORE I ASKED YOGI WHAT ALAN meant. Yogi sat and looked at me as if to decide whether to tell me the truth, tell me a joke, or tell me a lie. I realized I would discover the truth when his eyes watered and he glanced at the ground, full of shame. It seemed like shame.

He confessed to me that he had raped 75-100 women in Iwakuni, Japan. The Japanese government and Marine Corps were aware Yogi committed the crimes, but they couldn't prove it. None of the women could identify him as the rapist. They held him in a Japanese jail while they investigated to gather more evidence. He lived on rice and miso soup for weeks. The Japanese made a deal with the Marine Corps. The Marine Corps wanted Yogi out of the Japanese jail, to avoid any trouble with the Japanese government. Japanese authorities offered to release Yogi back to the Marine Corps only if they sent Yogi back to the United States. The Marine Corps agreed. They kept Yogi's transgressions a secret, gave him an "Undesirable Discharge," wrapped him up like a nice little package, and dumped him off in Oceanside, CA. Thanks for the gift.

When this awful truth hit me like a bullet in my heart, I sat there, frozen in disbelief. A choked sob escaped my mouth from somewhere deep inside. Then an all-out blubber arrived, where I couldn't contain myself. Yogi joined me. He told me it would never happen again and described how ashamed he was. He begged me to forgive him.

The idea of being alone petrified me. My mind played tricks on me, coaxing me to reason somehow that if he had me now, he wouldn't want sex from anyone else, and that he wouldn't rape anyone again as long as I was there for him. The school taught us it was Christ-like to forgive. I pushed this thought to the forefront of my mind when I decided to forgive Yogi. In retrospect, it was an excuse to stay with him so I wouldn't be alone. Unable to grasp how he got away with so many rapes, I quietly assured myself he must have been embellishing. This hideous, scary story seemed unbelievable. Yet, Alan drove three hours from the base to warn me about Yogi.

My vision of a rapist was of an ugly, creepy, crazed, and sex-starved maniac. Yogi didn't fit that description. Some parts of his story sounded as if he was even proud to have "outsmarted" the Japanese police, while still remorseful for all the horrific crimes he'd carried out. What kind of cabbagehead was I to believe all this? Could a person like this truly be sorry? Was it possible for a monster to change?

HANKERING TO PEEK

EVENTUALLY, THE PEACHTREE HOTEL invited us to leave for lack of payment. They held my suitcase hostage until I paid the bill in full. It turned out to be a recurring way of life for us in Atlanta. I was determined to hold on to my suitcase and not lose my family photo albums. All of my memories rested in my father's familiar brown suitcase. I didn't care about my clothes. Every few days I would remind the person at the counter of the old hotel, "Please don't throw my suitcase away. I will pay you all the money we owe." Yogi had nothing of value, no photographs, no memorabilia, he didn't even have any wonderful memories of his childhood and family. He didn't understand my desperation to get the suitcase back.

———

WE FOUND A PLACE TO RENT ON JUNIPER STREET. Our new spot was a single room in an old home with three or four rooms. They were small, and all the renters shared one bathroom. Our room had an old wooden door with a fluted glass doorknob. If you bent down and put your eye up to it, you could see everything in our room through the big keyhole. We put one of Yogi's socks on our side of the door to block anyone with the hankering to peek. The door had a transom window above it that was always open. One night we forgot our key. Yogi put me on his shoulders so I could crawl in through the window. I made it through about halfway and dived into our bed. Luckily, I didn't break my neck.

During a walk was the best time to talk with Yogi. He seemed receptive and shared more as his feet pounded the pavement.

"Tell me about your parents. We're going to visit, so I want to know all about them," I urged. Yogi's lighthearted face turned grim.

"There's not much to tell. My Ma loves her little dogs more than she loves anybody. She lets them shit all over the place and doesn't clean it up. My house is a real dump, you'll see."

Surprised, I asked him why. "There's something wrong with Ma. She's psychotic but won't see a doctor. Dad ignores her. I don't know why they adopted a kid and then treated him like shit."

And as quickly as he opened his box of tortured memories, he shut the lid just as fast. I noticed he had trouble talking about it. We walked on and Yogi returned to his jovial self. In reflection, his jovial self was a cover for the catacombs of darkness within him.

The magician must have waved his wand and uttered, "Abracadabra," because "poof," our money was gone. Neither of us had experience making or saving money.

Atlanta looked like Bakersfield on steroids. Yogi got a bright idea one night to emulate the local culture. The plan was to stand in front of the dirty movie theatre while Yogi posed as a hustler, pimping me to eager sexual deviants. There I stood in my blue jeans and purple floral halter top. At first it seemed like a game. I was unaware of how I should stand, or what my facial expression should be. How should a prostitute walk? It was too late to learn or practice any of their moves. I stood there, saucer-eyed with a giant smile plastered on my face, anticipating what would happen next.

A blue El Camino rolled up to the curb on Peachtree Street. In a quiet voice, and out of the side of his mouth, Yogi gave me instructions. "Act like you're going to the hotel but go home." He walked toward the blue car to talk to the man. The man stretched his neck out to watch me go by while his hungry eyes inspected my every move.

Yogi's plan was to pretend to set up a date with me and this guy and collect his money for the sex act. And just like that, my smile evaporated. Instead of sauntering like a hired hooker, I bolted down the street like a runaway truck. I ran toward the hotel, faster than I have every run in my life, then straight to our apartment. As I ran, a shady-looking guy driving by attempted to play my 'knight in shining armor'. As his car slowed, he rolled down the window. "Hey, you need a ride or something?" I did not stop. I kept running. "No! Get out of here! Go!" I yelled between gasps of air.

Not long after I made it back to our apartment, a disappointed Yogi strolled in. My bolting down the street ruined the deal and the guy in the El Camino drove off. Our pockets remained empty.

SPARE SOME CHANGE?

THE PEOPLE YOU LEAST EXPECT TO HELP YOU WHEN YOU ARE DOWN AND OUT are the ones doing the helping. Yogi and I would panhandle money for our meals. Those dressed for work would walk right past us and do everything in their power to avoid eye contact, for fear they might feel something.

One afternoon, I passed out from lack of food and water in front of a bar on Peachtree Street. Yogi picked me up and carried me inside. They offered me water and enough money to get to the hospital to see a doctor. The doctors checked me out and found out that simple hunger was the culprit. We returned to Peachtree Street.

We learned to stand near a restaurant and ask for money. The tallest woman I had ever seen strolled by us. She had to have been over six feet tall, without her stilettos. She sauntered by us, an average looking, slender Black woman with a ruby red smile and eye-catching gold hoop earrings that danced and dangled from her ears. I could see my reflection in the shine of her black patent purse. The potent scent of drug store perfume followed her when she passed. Yogi asked her if she could spare some change. She looked at us for a minute and with her ruby lips replied, "I'm fixing to get some breakfast so come on with me." We would see her now and again. She would stroll past us and say, "Come on," and wave us in. She never sat with us but would tell the server to get us anything we wished on the menu, and she would pay for it. We were always grateful.

———

YOGI GOT A POSITION at a print shop a few miles away. In the 70s, you would see many pages of help-wanted ads in the newspapers. It was the easiest way to find a job. He seemed at home in front of a letterpress. The shop sat on a gloomy street with few cars parked around it. The front door was a gigantic, filthy, metal garage door that rolled up. After the door rolled up, a heavy and rickety metal screen door opened and allowed you into the elevator. Dark and unsettling can only describe the cage. The sounds alone were enough to unnerve me. I could sense that I arrived when I was greeted by the sound of several presses moving, each printing something important for different clients. The smell of letterpress ink permeated throughout the entire shop, leaving me mildly intoxicated. The cleaning solvents used to clean a press is an odor you never forget.

Yogi got the night shift, which meant I would be alone in the apartment throughout the night. I explained my mother's security system of putting dishes and cups on a chair in front of the door when my dad worked out of town. Every evening Yogi left for work I dragged the old chair to the door and stacked our dishes, just so.

The East Area Rapist used the very same chair-and-dish technique for his security system. He began using this method on his sixteenth attack. It is believed he did this in case someone came in and caught him in the act. When the East Area Rapist broke into homes with couples, he had the female victim tie up the male. The rapist would then tie up the female. The EAR would stack dishes and cups on the male's back. He would move the female victim to another room to rape her. If the dishes rattled, he knew he had to check on the male.

———

OUR SEX LIFE SEEMED TO CHANGE when we were living in the studio apartment on Juniper Street. Maybe because his secrets were told, he didn't feel the need to hold back on anything. After all, he confessed to me his darkest, hair-raising secret, and I didn't leave him. He had a cabbagehead on his heels, following him through his horror story. I stayed because I was weak, alone, and scared. I was a frightened child who lost everything and accepted whatever came my way because I knew nothing else. He knew he had me.

Yogi suggested we pretend and act out some of our fantasies. This suggestion intrigued me. He had a fetish for women's undergarments. Though I owned just one pair of pants I had nearly forty pairs of panties and garter belts.

One night as I lay face down nude on our bed, Yogi straddled my body from behind and instructed me to, "Play with it. Play with my dick." I did, but it didn't seem practical in that position, and it made me uncomfortable, so I quit.

He whispered in my ear with his hot breath, "You're thirteen years old now. Do you like to fuck?"

I played along at first. "No, I'm thirteen years old! Thirteen-year-olds don't do this!"

Yogi then corrected his question, and asked me, "Have you ever fucked before?"

"No," I said.

I would like to say the rape game never happened again, but that would be a lie. I was going to let you believe that it didn't because I am ashamed of how blind I was. I didn't understand sex, and I didn't understand rape. A part of me knew it wasn't right, but I didn't understand just how wrong it was. Yogi had a blank canvas to create what he wanted to feed his sick mind. I was his canvas.

We relived his delusional fantasy sex game of rape from time to time. I was most always face down on the bed, no eye contact with him, and my arms behind my back to play with his penis. He asked me the same questions each time. His vocal demeanor resembled a person speaking to a little girl. In his fantasy, I was thirteen years old. The same words and questions the East Area Rapist used with his victims are the same words and questions Yogi used with me.

The act mirrored the rapes committed by the EAR, but I didn't wake from a deep sleep to a stranger with a flashlight and gun pointed at my head. I didn't shake in fear that my life would end. Shoelaces didn't tie my hands so tight that they turned purple. I didn't live in constant fear for decades. The East Area Rapist's victims did, though.

Often, I woke up to the blaring bedroom light and Yogi kissing my lips. He woke up, turned the light on, stared at me, then kissed me awake. It always startled me. I hoped he woke me up because he wanted me, but that wasn't the case. He would turn the light out and go to sleep. He woke me up just to enjoy the shocked expression on my face.

The East Area Rapist bound his victims' hands behind their backs. He rubbed lotion on his penis, placed it between their hands, and said:

Attacks #2, #5, #6, #12, #16, #17, #18, #21, #24, #26, #27, #36, #38, #41, #45, #46:

"Play with it."

"Play with my cock."

"Play with my dick."

"Stroke my cock."

"Rub it."

"Grab my cock and play with it."

He asked several victims the following questions:

Attack #9, #30, #42:

"Do you like to fuck?"

Attack #2 (age 16) #10 (age 15) #15 (age 16) #27 (age 12) #45 (age 17,) #47 (age 13):

"Have you ever fucked before?"

FLOWERPOT

ATLANTA WAS AN EYE-OPENING EXPERIENCE in that this is where I learned there were parts of the world much scarier and more dangerous than I ever imagined. "Server in a greasy spoon restaurant" was soon on my résumé. The manager drove me downtown and bought me a white uniform, since I didn't have the money. A pair of white panties should have been on that list. Bright, crazy colored panties were the only kind in my dresser drawer. Yogi raced to a secondhand store to look for a pair of tennis shoes for me.

My platform shoes broke, so I ran around barefoot at this point. I left the broken shoes in Piedmont Park. My heart felt like it left a bundled-up baby lying amid the leafy groundcover. I loved those shoes. It was a cabbagehead move for sure. It began to rain golden and peach-colored leaves, signaling fall had arrived. Walking barefoot in Georgia draped in California clothes in fall sent serious chills throughout my body.

Yogi returned with an enormous smile on his face and a bag with the ugliest Cardinal red colored pointy-toed tennis shoes I ever laid eyes on. Despite the embarrassing red tennis shoes that I had to wear, I was ready to start my new job. The jukebox played, "Living for The City" by Stevie Wonder in the background as I walked into work my first night.

The customers played that song so many times that I had it memorized in my head by the end of my first week. I could not remember a time when I was among such a diverse group of people. There sat a Black man wearing a wide brimmed purple hat drinking his coffee. A young Hispanic girl ate her biscuits and gravy with her right hand and read her papers with her left. A fuzzy-headed White guy wearing disheveled clothes stared at his water, while a few hookers laughed it up revisiting the previous night. Serving hoodlums, hustlers, pimps, bail bondsmen, prostitutes, and drug dealers became my livelihood.

People came and went from the restaurant as if it had a revolving door. Some ordered food and others just breezed in to talk with someone or use the restroom. It was a hub for all the criminals and the down-and-out to meet. When you entered, you heard a discord of loud music, cussing, and laughter. All eyes turned to look at you, deciding whether you were a friend or foe. The sound of burgers sizzling on a greasy grill, while two frazzled servers tried to keep up with it all, greeted me. It was comical to watch such a boisterous crowd disperse or become silent the moment law enforcement walked in to grab a bite to eat. The servers welcomed the silence.

A group of guys sitting on ripped-up orange stools gave me a nickname. Every time I turned around to grab a coffee cup, I heard them snicker. After ten minutes of this, one of them said, "We gonna call you Flowerpot!" They all laughed and wouldn't expand on why they gave me a silly nickname. Later, one of them named Fred filled me in on the joke. My panties with crazy, colored, enormous flowers bled right through the white seat of my pants. The nickname "Flowerpot" stuck with me. It became a term of endearment by all the regulars.

Fred, a small guy with a head full of braids roaming every which way carried himself with confidence. He wore a genuine smile with a glittery gold tooth that peeked out. He was the only person I met with an actual name, and I bet that wasn't really his name. All the regulars respected him. I wondered if he was an undercover cop or the head dope dealer or someone you didn't want to irritate. Fred became my friend and looked out for me from that time until we left Atlanta. Fred must have figured me out early, just like the cafe owner in Bakersfield.

I shivered on those chilly dark mornings when I had to walk home after serving it up to the less-than-stellar clientele at that old 24-hour diner. Fred said, "Come on. Let's get you a coat." I walked right along with no fear of him or where he was leading me. We walked a long way down Peachtree Street.

Without warning, Fred shouted, "Get down! Get down now!" He pushed me down to the ground. Yells came from across the street. A police officer struggled to catch a man running. The officer's gun was out of his holster. I was so glad Fred paid attention to the opposite side of the street. I had my eyes to the ground, searching for dimes.

We arrived at our destination, which ended up being a dark shanty. The street was motionless, and all I heard was the sound of dogs yapping in backyards. Fred fumbled for his keys because the porch light was out. He unlocked the solid front door and to my surprise; we entered what looked like a professional's home. I stood there amazed as my eyes roamed the stunning living room. Beautiful furniture, perfectly arranged, and plenty of bookshelves lined with books. His home was immaculate.

I wanted to ask him who he really was, but I learned early that living on the streets nothing is my business unless I am told. When we entered the bedroom, he flung the closet doors open. There must have been ten women's jackets neatly hanging in a row. He looked at a few and chose the jacket with the fake fur around the collar. It was the one I would have picked for myself. He shut the closet door, and we left. I wondered whose closet we just invaded. Did it belong to a girlfriend or one of his working girls? Either way, someone would miss a jacket, but my body was toasty warm, thanks to Fred.

After combing through a secondhand store, an adorable Wrangler jean jacket called out to me. When I wore that jacket, I thought I looked so cool. It meant even more because I saved my tips from the greasy spoon restaurant to buy it. I wore it everywhere, even if I wasn't cold. One evening, a commotion started brewing. Everyone in our apartment left to go outside to check out the situation. Several police cars went by with sirens screaming and lights flashing. It drew other people from other homes and apartments outside. The flurry of excitement came and left.

The next morning when I woke up, I reached for my jean jacket. It just walked off by itself, I suppose. I searched the entire apartment, but it was nowhere to be found. I replayed the previous evening in my mind over and over. The jacket always landed on the same chair, where I always left it at the end of the day. Someone stole my little Wrangler! That's the only explanation. A few weeks later I moseyed into work and Fred held my jean jacket up in the air on one of his fingers. A prostitute had come into the greasy spoon late that night, ordered a cup of coffee, and pulled my driver's license out of the jean jacket pocket. Fred recognized my photo and retrieved the license and my favorite little jean jacket. I could see the good in Fred, and I still smile when he crosses my mind.

A couple of extra bucks in our pocket one night led us to a few shabby little bars on Peachtree Street. The first seedy bar you walk into makes you want to check your glass for lipstick marks. After the third place you visit, you're willing to drink from someone's old shoe.

The drinking age was eighteen in Georgia. Drinking was new to me, and I wasn't sure I liked it yet, but Yogi encouraged me. I chose the prettiest drink I ever laid eyes on: the Sloe Gin Fizz. It reminded me of the Shirley Temple drinks I had when I was little. It was not only a vibrant pink color, but sweet and mighty tasty. It was also easy to gulp down, which I did. I felt the fuzzy warmness it gave me. Yogi was happy just slurping his Coors beers and wiping the froth from his mustache after every sip.

Little did I know we were in a state that belonged to the Confederates.

I wished I paid more attention to those history classes. Three young Georgian men sat across from us at a small table. They had been there awhile, judging by their posture. They seemed to slide out of their chairs like noodles sliding off a fork. A couple of empty pitchers rested on the plastic red and white checkered tablecloth. The ashtrays were brimming over, full of cigarettes that were smoked down to the filters.

Yogi had two settings, loud and louder. To be quite honest, I'm sure he wanted everyone to listen to what he had to say. We drank like fish and laughed like loons. I caught the guys across from us glaring and staring in our direction. Were our voices too loud? No one else seemed to care.

"Hey, Blue Belly. Why don't you shut your fucking mouth?" one blurted out. Yogi just stared at the guy. "Yeah, fucking Yankee," another chimed in. I wanted to take in a deep breath to relax, but I was afraid to move. My eyes darted about while my legs shook. I prepared myself to witness a fight.

Yogi sat up a little straighter in his chair and folded his hands together on the table like a schoolboy. He rattled off the most interesting details of the American Civil War. "What the hell is happening here?" I questioned myself. With raised brows, the young men's eyes widened as they grabbed their jackets and left in a blur. They must have thought Yogi was nuts, just like I did.

Yogi explained how his New England accent gave away the fact that he came from a Union State. He enlightened me to the fact that "Blue Belly" was a derogatory name for a northern soldier. This marked a history lesson I never forgot. His ingenuity of discussing the war thwarted a fight. Yogi explained, "If you're ever in a situation you think you can't get out of, start acting crazy. People don't know how to react to someone who's unpredictable." I never forgot that advice.

I learned more history from Yogi than I did in all my history classes. Nice to see his knowledge of history paid off, even if it turned into a bizarre situation. We left the bar only to find another one down the street. My words slurred, and I required a little help to get from Point A to Point B; and still, the Sloe Gin Fizzes kept coming.

We stumbled out of the bar and down the sidewalk until we found ourselves in front of a "peep show." Yogi wanted to show me what they were all about. Particle boards separated the handmade booths. They painted them black to hide the dirt and filth left behind by the customers. The nickels, dimes, and quarters trickled into the machines, and there was an overall clinking sound that reverberated throughout the building. The sound was a reminder that I was surrounded by perverts in their nasty little booths. It was minimal privacy to those plinking in their quarter to watch the short pornographic movie and masturbate. The way it worked was that the movie would stop at a critical point, and you would have to put in more quarters to keep watching. Yogi tossed in a few quarters.

Beads of sweat lined my forehead and upper lip. My legs begged for something to hold me up. The room swirled like a tornado as Yogi laid me down on the cold cement floor. I was three sheets to the wind, as he would say. He pulled down my jeans and panties to my ankles. My butt cheeks felt the stinging cold cement floor. He lay on top of the lower half of my body and began fucking me. My hands curled into fists, and I hit his shoulders over and over. My fists slamming against him made no difference. "Get off me!" I yelled. "Stop it! Get off now! Let's go!" Over and over the words came out of my mouth slower and slower. If yelling louder would have been possible, I still don't think anyone there would have bothered to help me.

Yogi stood me up and pulled up my pants. Fury raged throughout every fiber of my being. Hot tears ran down my face and humiliation overpowered my drunkenness. Unable to speak, I walked without saying a word. We made it back to the apartment, and we both slept until the next afternoon.

In the shower, I scrubbed every inch of my body until my skin turned dark pink and ached. I stood there and let the warm soapy water wash away my shame. Yogi laid me on a filthy floor full of countless men's sperm and raped me. He took something that didn't belong to him because he wanted it. I couldn't get clean enough.

I was silent for most of the next day. When I did speak, I called him every filthy word I knew. I sounded like an auctioneer, only I spewed cuss words. He apologized over and over and blamed it all on being drunk that night. "A person won't do anything drunk they wouldn't do if they were sober." These were Yogi's words to me in Bakersfield. *God, Helen! Were you listening?*

The only girlfriend I had in Atlanta was a man named April. April had a few years on me. She resembled a very feminine woman, pretty, full of life, with a colorful personality. But she was every bit of a man. We laughed and giggled together like girlfriends do. Every weekend we would put outfits together for her to wear that night. I would help her with her makeup and watch her walk in her silver sparkly heels. She would put a fluffy blonde wig on her head, and I would tell her she looked prettier than Marilyn Monroe. I would help her style the wig to her perfection. She tucked her junk in her bikini panties and was ready to work the streets. She would stroll down the stairs each night. The sound of her high heels clicking the steps let you know it was 9:00 p.m., the time she left each night. By morning she returned with delicious breakfast and cigarettes for us. Yogi didn't like her at all but that didn't stop him from diving into a stack of pancakes or lighting up a Marlboro that she brought us.

April snuck into my heart. She was easy to love because she was fun and playful and had a giving soul. But she suffered extreme pain, and she often shared it with me. I would listen, hoping to make her pain go away, but it never did. It seemed much too heavy for me to carry. She spoke of things I knew nothing about. She would tell me stories of her father getting her drunk and raping her. Her mother refused to help her, so she ran away in her early teens and lived on the streets. She learned she could make money turning tricks for what she called, "Chicken

Hawks." These were older men who wanted to have sex with younger males. I didn't understand why she repeated her own horrific history. One evening while brushing her hair, April grabbed me and tried to kiss me. I turned the hairbrush around and stabbed her with the rat tail end. "Get the hell away from me! I thought you wanted to be a girl!" I shouted. April moved away soon after that episode. I missed her.

THE TIP OF HIS KNIFE

I LEARNED NOT TO GET ATTACHED TO PEOPLE, PLACES, OR THINGS. It became important for survival. My upbringing had been more of a trusting one. This unfamiliar world disturbed me. Yogi was comfortable living in survival mode. In fact, he reveled in it. He seemed to fit right in with all the slime oozing its way around, consuming its prey. These people were sly, and if they wanted something you had, they would get it. Atlanta reminds me of the song, *Smiling Faces Sometimes,* by The Temptations.

On the nights Yogi wasn't working, he would leave the house to go for a walk, always just before bedtime. His behavior left me annoyed. I tried to stay awake as long as possible but would almost always fall asleep waiting for him. It bothered me that he didn't want to go to sleep at the same time I did. I feared the bogeyman would get me while I was alone at night. No matter how much I complained about his nighttime walks, he ignored them and continued. Sometimes when he came in, I would peek at the clock. Usually, the next morning when I asked him when he came in the night before, he always gave a time much earlier than what I saw on the clock.

I was returning from work one day when I saw a clean-cut young man walking my way. He sauntered along at a slow pace. He stopped me as I approached my walkway and asked where he could find the grocery store. While I gave him directions, he moved closer to me. It was much too close, and it violated my space. My inside alarm was going off, but I couldn't think fast enough to get away. Hesitating, I worried more about what he would think if I moved and not enough about my safety.

He wrapped his arm around me and held a knife to my throat. "Start walking nice and slow to your place. Is anybody home?" I squeaked out a "No," and walked to the entrance door. Anyone who might have been watching us walk up to my door would have seen me and a guy with his arm around me. The tip of his metal knife resting on my neck was unmistakable. My heart wanted to stop and beat fast at the same time. I trembled in fear, unable to speak.

He opened the front door. "Which apartment is yours?" The building was an older home with three apartments inside that shared a bathroom. Our apartment had two doors. We padlocked the first door. Yogi lost the key so we would leave the second door unlocked. I walked with the man up to the padlocked door and stood still. I tried to stall in hopes of a neighbor walking out and seeing us, but that didn't happen. He growled and said in a barely audible voice, "This ain't your apartment," and put the tip of his knife into my neck, pressing it, almost breaking the skin. I thought to myself, I am going to die today.

I walked him back to the second door that was unlocked. He pushed me in and let me go. I stood there in shock, waiting for his next move. He looked at me and said, "I left my beer on your porch, go get it." This never made sense to me. If his primary motive was to burglarize my apartment, he was in for an enormous surprise. The only money he might come across would have been about 75 cents hidden in the cap of my hairspray can. I didn't care. I was going to follow his orders.

I ran outside so fast my feet didn't touch the ground. I never knew I could fly. Reaching the greasy spoon was my only goal. Fred's face is the first one I recognized. I blurted out, "Help!" It was the only word I could get out of my mouth. Unable to tell him what happened, I slowed down to catch my breath. He got on the phone and called the police. I waited for hours, and no one came to take a report or find the perpetrator. I gave up and walked all the way to Yogi's printing job to tell him what happened. He screamed and yelled so loud and high that the older deaf woman wrote on a piece of paper and handed it to me, "I thought I was deaf!"

The police arrived in the morning to take a report. They were familiar with who I described to them and wanted me to help set him up in a cocaine bust. They told me he sold cocaine on the strip. I looked at the officers as if they asked me the meaning of life in Japanese. I came unhinged and yelled at the cops. "Are you kidding me? I don't know this man! He held a knife to my throat, planned to rape me, and you want me to help you get him for selling cocaine?" I guess they must have thought that if I was living among them, I must be one of them. They made it seem like rape was just a four-letter word, not to be repeated. I wanted out of this armpit of the devil I lived in.

———

FRED DROVE US TO THE AIRPORT TO FINALLY LEAVE GEORGIA. We bought tickets to Boston. Don't ask me where we got the money. Fred told us he was glad to see us leave. I was eager to meet the person Yogi called, "Ma," or so I thought.

LEVEE WALKS AND TRAIN TRACK TALKS 1975

MY EARS POPPED AS THE PLANE DESCENDED. AT THAT
POINT, WE DIDN'T care if we had to jump out before landing. The
flight was like a bad bumper car ride. Yogi grabbed my father's old
brown Samsonite suitcase filled with the few things we owned. It was
January and Boston was wrapped in a white icy shawl. I felt warm in
the coat Fred gave me in Atlanta.

We caught a cab to downtown Boston and ended up in the Combat
Zone. It catered to those searching for adult entertainment. It got its
name in the 1960s. Sailors and soldiers being shipped off from the
Boston Navy Yard rendezvoused in the Combat Zone before leaving.
There were so many dressed in their uniforms, it looked like a combat
zone. High crime, prostitution, strip clubs, nude go-go dancers, peep
shows, and X-rated theaters riddled the district. Yogi told me everything
bad that happened went on right there. The adult district oozed police
corruption and organized crime. The Wall Street Journal described it
as a "sexual Disneyland."

An assortment of degenerates walked up and down those streets.
They didn't even hide the fact their eyes bore holes through you as they

sauntered by. They sized you up to see why you were there. Sad to say, my first glimpse of Boston wasn't the best. For a minute, I thought we flew in a circle and landed back in Atlanta.

We spent the night in a cheap hotel, of course. The sun wasn't up yet, so we slept a while before calling his dad for a ride. I slept in and woke up to an older man standing there in his wrinkled baggy pants gaping at me. Yogi introduced him as his dad. It was a good thing since my eyes refused to focus. I tried to be cordial and excused myself to the bathroom.

Half-awake and a little ticked off, I splashed my face with water and got dressed. I couldn't believe Yogi invited his dad in where I slept and introduced us when my hair looked like I pulled it out of a mixer. My dragon breath shot out 10 feet, I'm sure. After I got ready, we all drove to breakfast. My head stayed down for a few minutes until the embarrassing moment left me and the coffee did its job.

The only one talking in the car was Yogi. His father only had about two words to say. How weird was that? They hadn't seen each other for a long time. I sat in the back seat, just as quiet as his dad. Yogi blabbed on about everything. He had a one-way conversation, except for a few head nods from his father.

When we turned down Yogi's street, the only thing I heard was breathing. It was like someone found Yogi's off button. The neighborhood conjured up old memories. Or maybe he was preparing himself to see his Ma. Yogi hadn't spoken to her since he left for Japan. His parents knew about the crimes he committed and knew the Marine Corps gave him an undesirable discharge.

The front door opened only halfway, and I could hear the shrillness of his mother's voice that stabbed me deep into my eardrum. She called out his name, his real name. It was the first time I heard anyone say it. There she stood, a short, plump, gray-haired woman with a messy bun balancing on her head, snapping and cracking her chewing gum. It looked as though someone pulled out all her teeth, shuffled them, then put them back in the wrong place. I stood smiling, anticipating my introduction. My legs were ready to bolt in case she insulted me. After all, Yogi told me a few stories about her; none of them good. Yogi introduced us and we exchanged hellos. She seemed more pleasant than I expected.

I pictured a different home altogether. An old, small, two-story house is where Yogi grew up. Inside, every corner of the home had something pushed aside or crammed in it. Stacks of papers, mail, and coupons took up every square inch of every table. These stacks of papers didn't just happen. They had been laying there for years. My eyes roamed, trying to find a clean spot, but no such luck. Useless objects were as far as the eye could see. Mustiness and dust filled my nostrils. The wooden floors creaked, and they looked as though a herd of cats used them as a scratching post. Old wallpaper clung on to the walls for dear life.

I never entered the room off the kitchen. I had to peek, though. Meant to be a dining room, this is the room his Ma used as the dog poop room. Newspapers covered the old stained wooden floor. The papers laid out on the floor, even though the dogs left about the same time Yogi left. Yogi had been away for quite some time. Why did the old newspapers still cover the dining room floor? It was a mystery to me, a disgusting mystery.

Yogi and I stayed with his parents for a short time. He slept upstairs in his old bedroom, and I got to sleep on the couch downstairs. If they only knew what went on between us before we got there, they might not have cared too much about our sleeping arrangements. First thing each morning, I had to relive my first introduction to his dad. There he sat reading the newspaper, drinking his coffee just a few feet away. I covered my head and face with the blanket and pretended to be asleep until Yogi came downstairs.

Neither of his parents seemed happy to see Yogi. I imagined under the circumstances they had to be sad and disappointed in the bouncing baby son they adopted. Yogi's father and brother both served in the Navy and had "Honorable Discharges." They, at one time, had hoped Yogi would join the Navy, too. Yogi had been a soldier on his own mission.

The white house, weathered and chipped from the harsh Massachusetts winters, sat a few doors down from an old factory. Beyond the factory were train tracks. The tracks led around all the nearby neighborhoods. Yogi and I took long walks on the tracks for something to do. He had been walking the same tracks since he was a young boy.

On the train tracks is where he smoked his weed and reflected. "Yeah, I got caught peeking in windows and burglarizing homes right down there," he said, as he pointed down to a cluster of homes. "I was only fifteen and a half." Between tokes on his joint and a cough here and there, he revealed a secret to me. "I would do whatever and when I finished, I'd climb right back up on the tracks and be in another town before the cops ever got to the house and found out what happened." Innocently, I thought, *I'm so glad he stopped all that.*

"They sealed my record when I turned eighteen." We passed a newer looking apartment building. "The same thing there," he said as he stared at the buildings until they were out of view. After he told me about the apartments, he looked relieved. He laughed aloud as if I told him a hilarious joke, then he changed the subject. Did he just walk me down his memory lane?

I didn't understand what was funny. I chalked it up to him trying to break the seriousness of it all. Was he more than a voyeur in his younger years?

———

The East Area Rapist chose homes that backed up to fields, ditches, or levees to make a quick getaway from his crimes. He waited on train tracks, stalking his next victims. His reconnaissance missions were meticulous and lengthy.

When I read how the EAR would get away, I thought back to this very moment. Yogi learned early on how to position himself to pull out from an area where he just stole someone's joy and peace of mind.

Recently I spoke to one of Yogi's old friends from his hometown and I revealed some of the details in the book I was writing. His friend, without hesitation, told me he remembered a time Yogi boasted about driving his maroon Chevy to Boston over the weekend, he said he picked up a girl and raped her. He and Yogi were about seventeen or eighteen years old at the time. Of course, his friend didn't believe it at the time. He couldn't believe him. Who wants to think their friend is a rapist? He went on to tell me that Yogi made many trips to Boston before joining the Marines.

It got me thinking about the walk we took on the train tracks long ago. The apartment complexes we passed by... his talk about his unspecified deeds... were these crimes worse than what he had alluded to? When did this horror story really begin? He first admitted to his friend that he raped a girl when he was seventeen and admitted to me that there were seventy-five or more women in Japan. How many women did he rape in Boston? In Oceanside? In Bakersfield? In Los Angeles? In Atlanta? Sacramento? And everywhere else in between?

Yogi's parents were an older couple with much older children. They adopted him from a family friend when he was an infant. Sherri, his adoptive sister, was eight years older. Yogi told me on one of our train-track talks that when he was young, his sister would walk around in her panties while she got ready to go somewhere. While telling me the story, his lips tightened, his teeth clenched, and he shook. Agitated, he pinned the blame on Sherri. He acted the same way when he told me about the Japanese women in Iwakuni. I can only determine from his behavior that Sherri aroused him, or he got in trouble for staring or peeking at her. Or the unthinkable. Whichever the case, that subject hit one of his raw nerves.

Yogi's Ma, Janet, belittled him every chance she got. I suppose she figured out if she ended her degrading sentences with a giggle, it wouldn't seem so bad. Her ear-splitting voice made it worse.

One morning Yogi helped his parents bring the groceries into the house. He carried too many paper bags in his hands. I'm sure he tried to look strong or hoped to cut down on his trips to the old car outside. One bag ripped down the side as he sat it on the kitchen table. Cans of green beans and corn fell to the dirty floor and rolled around until the metal chair legs stopped them.

Janet squealed, "The bag broke because you're so stupid! Jesus, you're stupid." His Ma emphasized "stupid." She laughed, pretending to be joking. His dad plodded along with the other bags and ignored everything as if nothing happened. No facial expression at all.

I got the notion that Yogi's father gave up speaking altogether. He ignored us almost the entire time we stayed there. His dad was retired but kept himself busy by reading the newspaper whenever we came around. How long did it take to read a newspaper, anyway? Did he read that paper or was it a prop to avoid talking with us?

"Would you like to take a walk to the coffee shop with me? I need a walk and a hot cup of coffee right now." Yogi's father looked at his brother, but never looked at Yogi. His brother didn't even look at him. They didn't invite him. For a few seconds Yogi's eyes dropped and with lips pursed he let out a big breath of air. And with that, Yogi and I took our own stroll on the train tracks again.

"Wow! What was that all about back there?" I asked.

"It's been like that my whole life," he said.

"It surprised me since your dad and brother haven't seen you in a long time."

"Yeah." Yogi inhaled another hit from a joint as we hiked down the tracks. He walked the tracks at a good clip; I noticed a vacant look in his watery blue eyes.

We stayed a short time at his parents, then we wore our welcome out at his brother's home. I understood how Yogi got his name. He ate everything in sight without asking. One time I found a pink box of donuts in the dryer. His poor sister-in-law was at her wit's end. She had to hide the box of donuts from him.

"Fuck them if they can't take a joke," Yogi liked to say.

———

YOGI FOUND WORK AT ANOTHER LOCAL PRINT SHOP, and I started work at a large discount store as a cashier. Our next temporary home was a city away. It was a two-story, four-bedroom house that sat on a nice sized piece of property. We rented a small upstairs room and had about three other guys as housemates. The guys were mellow and easy to get along with. Yogi knew a few of them already, so it was a comfortable situation.

The street name was Stone Street. We all called it Stoned Street, which fit since most everyone who visited got stoned. It was the joke back then. One evening, the guys had a big party. Earlier, I left my favorite Wrangler jean jacket on the chair. The next morning, I came downstairs to find it missing. You guessed it. Stolen twice. It made my eyes well up. The only thing stopping me from crying was my anger. What makes everyone think they can take other people's personal property? I didn't want to be a baby about it, but the jacket meant a lot to me. To get the jacket back a second time would be a miracle, I thought. My roommate's eyebrows lifted as he stared at me. He was a gentle giant who soared over me in height. The bushiest beard clung to his face. He told me not to worry. I saw the wheels turning, and he told me he remembered who might have left with it on. That night he returned with it hanging over his arm and had a smile the size of Massachusetts. My lucky Wrangler jacket! The jacket hangs in my closet today.

In the beginning, Yogi had many friends, and all were happy to see him. It had been a couple of years since he lived at home. His one close friend grew up and lost interest in their friendship. Although, a couple of nights at the neighborhood bar drew a crowd, as they enjoyed Yogi's entertainment factor. Soon the welcome wagon disappeared. It's possible they realized he hadn't changed. The class clown still lacked drive. Or maybe his friends found out the real reason his time in the service was cut short.

Along another levee walk, Yogi divulged to me his adopted father beat him with a dog chain, while his brother watched. The visual of the story was too much to bear. My mouth dropped open as I grabbed his hand to comfort him. I didn't ask him why. There just couldn't be a good enough reason. I often wondered how different his life could have been if he got help when he was young.

We agreed when we arrived, that we couldn't wait to leave. Yogi realized coming home turned out to be a big mistake. We scraped and saved every dime. I should say I scraped and saved every dime I had to get back home. That's where my heart was. "There won't be anyone there to call you stupid, play mind games, beat you with dog chains, or anything else," I promised. Yogi crammed all that inside him and carted it along with us like an overstuffed backpack. Now and then those ugly memories rose from that backpack and all hell would break loose.

1974 OCEANSIDE, CA. 18 YEARS OLD

1975 In the kitchen of Yogi's mother's house. I turned 20 that year.

THE BLUE APARTMENTS, 2021. IN THE 70S THE BODY OF THE BUILDING WAS LIGHT BLUE, AND THE TRIM COLOR WAS A DARKER BLUE. IT'S ACROSS THE STREET FROM THE CA DEPT. OF VETERANS AFFAIRS BUILDING. WE LIVED IN THE LEFT CORNER APARTMENT UPSTAIRS.

1975   1228 O Street, Sacramento, CA. Inside the Blue Apartments
I'm in front of our lovely living room curtains.

Yogi in 1981 and one composite of the East Area Rapist 3-4 yrs. earlier. This composite is one of three used by the FBI in 2016 to aid the public in finding the EAR.

1818 P STREET, SACRAMENTO, CA., 2021

38ᵀᴴ Street, Sacramento, CA., 2021. Behind the
duplex is the detached wooden garage.

FEBRUARY 1980. YOGI AND I ATTENDED THOMAS AND MARY'S WEDDING

FRONT PAGE OF YOGI'S BIRTHDAY CARD TO ME

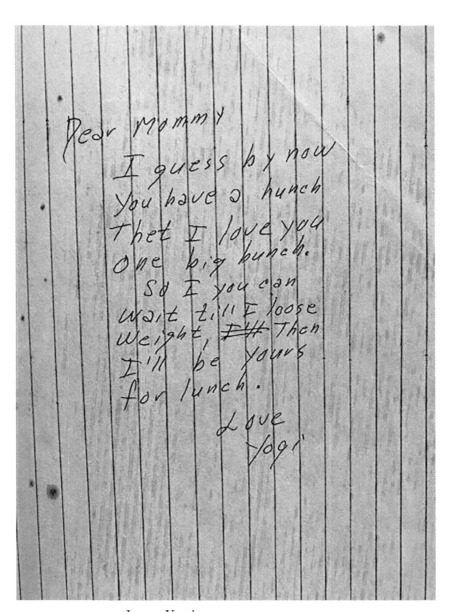

INSIDE YOGI'S BIRTHDAY CARD TO ME

GENERAL CUSTER ESSAY

SIMILARITIES BETWEEN GENERAL CUSTER ESSAY AND THE BIRTHDAY CARD I SEE ARE:

S= THE PRINTED "S" IN SUIX

T= A SHORT CROSS ON THE RIGHT

G= STRAIGHT TAIL

Y= THE PRINTED "Y" IN "CHEYNRE" AND YOGI.

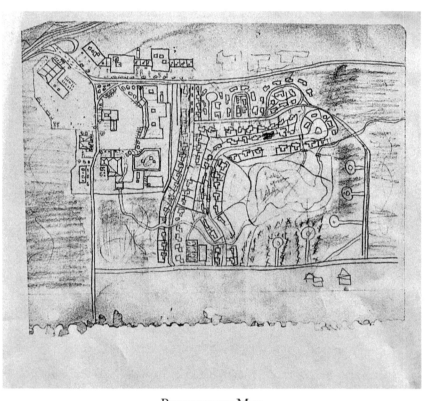

PUNISHMENT MAP

PART 4

PIECES TO THE PUZZLE

THE BLUE
APARTMENTS 1975

A SUDDEN FLARE OF JOY LIT INSIDE ME AS WE GOT CLOSER TO RETURNING to Sacramento. Too many years had passed since Aunt Ruby plucked me from my hometown. No one warned me it wouldn't be the same. And it couldn't be, anyway, because my mother wasn't there. Friends grew up just like me and lived scattered around town with jobs and families.

I was 20 years old. It was a fresh start for Yogi and me and we tried to embrace it. Sacramento hadn't changed too much. I only knew it from a child's perspective, though. In 1975 the city was a haven of sorts, for the vilest, most wretched criminals: The serial rapists. I believe they're just one step below murderers. Forty-five years ago, most people didn't look at it this way. There were a few of them running amuck in the Sacramento area. Too many women endured rapes in the 70s with few arrests. The ones caught spent little time in prison. When they were let out, they returned to doing the same thing that put them in jail.

Yet, Yogi and I seemed oblivious to all the crimes taking place around Sacramento. Our heads were in the clouds. We had made it to my childhood home, and that's what mattered to us. We took a bus ride from the airport to downtown Sacramento.

"Take a deep breath, Yogi. That's my hometown, Sacramento, that you're smelling." We shuffled our way through all the other bus riders to reach our luggage.

"Smells like bus exhaust to me." He lifted our suitcases from the terminal, and we were on our way.

With suitcases in hand, we made our way to the Berry Hotel. It was built in 1929. The hotel thrived among the best department stores, ornate movie theatres, and other hotels in the downtown area. Considered a luxury hotel then, in the 70s it was nothing more than a flophouse. The shabby hotel was home for us for one night and one night only, and it was a sleepless night. Other hotel guests slammed doors and yelled in the hallways all night long. If I didn't know better, I would have thought the carnival came to the Berry Hotel with game barkers and loud side shows.

"Yogi, Yogi, wake up. There's something going on outside our door."

"It's just a bunch of speed freaks who don't know what time it is," he said, then rolled over, taking all the covers with him.

We found an apartment in no time. The apartment manager held his stethoscope to our chests, listened for a heartbeat, and in less than a minute we stood the proud renters at The Blue Apartments. I felt sure if I put my hand on the bed, it would still be warm from the last renter. The place didn't have a name, just an address, so we called our new home The Blue Apartments. If a building could talk, this one would have screamed, "Help me. I'm so ugly." The paint store owners must have smiled to see the buckets full of their hideous blue paint leave the store. The body color of the building was a lighter blue and the trim color a darker blue. I could guarantee our new place was not the envy of the town.

They furnished our new home with old worn furniture, a lumpy bed, and a few pots and pans in the compact kitchen. In Georgia, we had rented rooms in older homes and shared bathrooms with other renters. I remember one had a bathtub, but no shower. Someone showed some ingenuity and cut a green garden hose, about twelve inches long, and attached it to the bathtub spout with wire. You either sat or squatted in the tub to use the hose as a shower if you didn't want your skin to touch the dirty tub.

The Blue Apartments' bathroom looked fabulous to us compared to the other bathrooms we endured. We didn't have to share it with other people. Tattered blue and pink curtains hung in the living room and looked so tired of hanging there. The curtains hadn't seen soap and water for some time. We still used them for the backdrop of many of our photos. A ragged musty smelling carpet remnant covered part of the stained wooden floor. I always wondered what the carpet covered up but was too afraid to peek.

There were two views out our windows. One view from the kitchen stared straight into the other blue building next door. If my arms were a little longer, I could have shaken my neighbor's hand. The view from the front window was a little more interesting, where we could see the State of California Veterans Affairs building and their parking lot. Our apartment was at the front of the building on the second floor above the apartment entrance door. Every day we watched people come and go from the Veterans Affairs building until it all halted at 5:00 p.m. The workers scattered like wild horses and within minutes 13th and O Street returned to its original state again; still and quiet.

The East Area Rapist attacked plenty of victims who were connected to the military.

I can't help but wonder if Yogi screened some of his victims through our living room window as military personnel and veterans came and went from the Veterans Affairs Building right in front of us.

The common hallway of the apartments smelled of old sweat and whiskey. Sacramento summer heat would compound the horrible odor. We plugged our noses and tried to make it up the stairs to our apartment before we took another breath. By the time we made it inside, I gasped for fresh air. Yogi skipped steps to beat me to the door. I would laugh and tell him, "You are going to split your pants doing that." He reminded me of a gazelle, not an enormous animal, but swift and known for running and jumping high when a predator comes near.

Yogi's primary exercise was walking. He was a grazing couch potato inside the house. Outside, he was a marching kind of guy, focused only on his destination. The Marine Corps influenced his physical bearing and pace. With all the walking he did, Yogi stayed in great shape. His thighs were muscular, and his legs were firm. He always stood with his hands on his hips. It was his usual stance. I wondered if the Marine Corp taught him to take up as much space as possible to show dominance while he worked as a military police officer.

———

The East Area Rapist was described as agile and physically fit with muscular thighs. He easily bound fences, crossed ditches and fields to escape law enforcement after his attacks. He was quick enough to avoid getting caught even when helicopters and tracking dogs were unleashed to find him.

———

We made friends with a couple our age that lived across the hall from us. I should say I made friends with them. Yogi didn't like either of them. Her name was Betty. Betty grew up living with her father, who drove long-haul trucks for a living. She was a no-nonsense kind of girl. Betty didn't stand for any bullshit from anyone, and I admired her for that. Gregarious, protective, and street-smart are the best words to describe Betty. I liked her the minute we met. I think I've always been drawn to stronger people… unless they tried to control me.

Our money vanished quickly and that encouraged us to find work in a hurry. It wouldn't be long before rent and utilities were due again. We got the hang of how monthly bills worked. No sooner did you pay them, they magically reappeared again. Yogi and I looked through our closet to find something to wear to a job interview.

We arrived with our suitcases bulging and had enough clothes to sort and hang in our closet for once. I had dresses, tops, and pants I bought at a discount store where I worked in Massachusetts. Yogi had an assortment of clothing and shoes but preferred wearing his military fatigues and black lace-up boots. He swore it was the most comfortable clothing to wear. He found an Army/Navy store in Sacramento and bought plain green and camouflage shirts and pants.

In the 70s, some guys wore military clothing, so most people didn't consider it odd. I thought it was strange. I wouldn't wear a nurse's uniform or a police officer's uniform just because it was comfortable. Yogi didn't mind looking as if he just walked off a battlefield. As much as Yogi was disappointed with the Marine Corp, he still wanted to look and feel the part of being associated with them. Yogi wore his fatigues and boots when he took long walks in the late evenings.

The East Area Rapist wore military fatigues and black combat boots to some of the earlier attacks.

The front door opened, and Yogi skipped across the floor doing a little dance. His hips twisted and turned. I wanted to laugh but didn't dare spoil his mood. He smiled so hard all I could see were about thirty teeth in front of me.

"What? Good news?" I managed to ask.

"Guess."

"I don't know. Just tell me, please. I hate guessing."

"Chotto matte kudasai (*Wait a minute*, in Japanese), you are talking to someone who is an offset pressman. I start tomorrow."

"Oh, I am so happy and proud of you. That didn't take long at all."

We sat and described all the food we would buy with his first paycheck. Big fat juicy steaks, real lunch meat for sandwiches, gallons of fresh cold milk, and of course ice-cold Coors beer for Yogi. Click, click, click was the sound Yogi's teeth made. He had a habit of clicking his teeth when he became excited or engrossed in thought. It sounded as if he was chewing something into teeny tiny pieces. We both grinned from ear to ear that entire day. But I soon learned nothing lasts forever.

Yogi was employed and part of me hated it. I didn't get along with myself when I was alone. Surrounded by people for so many years, it was hard to get used to hearing my own thoughts and enjoying silence.

There were no peepholes in the thin doors at The Blue Apartments. It was impossible to pretend you weren't home. That's exactly what I wanted to do when Yogi was away. Every so often I heard tapping at the door. I froze in place and didn't move a muscle. I knew who it was.

The Blue Apartments had its own resident heroin addict. Yogi befriended him with idle chat and cigarettes from time to time. Willie was his name. He was a skinny, disheveled man in his late sixties. His tiny pupils, rotten teeth, and erratic behavior scared me.

Sometimes if you looked out the living room window at the right time you could watch Willie dance and yell in front of the apartments. The area was vacant, but he was yelling at someone. "Leave me alone you bastard! Get away from me!" he would say. Now and then you could see the front of his pants were wet from urine.

Willie would stop by to ask for a cigarette, and Yogi always complied. Willie got mad if you didn't give him one. I always hated it when Yogi was gone.

Tap, tap, tap. Tap, tap, tap. Willie made a ruckus at the door.

"I know you're in there," he'd say. "I need a cigarette real bad."

There was no way I was going to open the door to appease him. I stayed quiet for at least an hour and regulated my breathing to short silent breaths.

When my thoughts turn back to The Blue Apartments, I think of Willie.

He represented the type of people who lived there. The lost, the hungry drug addicts, prostitutes, poor people, and us. Willie could have been the Mayor of The Blue Apartments.

Yogi was always a welcome sight. It seemed I was always frightened when I was by myself. I know my fear didn't come close to the fear felt by the women the East Area Rapist attacked.

Well, that job didn't last long. Yogi got fired more times than a cannonball. Sometimes he couldn't last long enough to pick up his first paycheck. He worked at so many different places as a dishwasher, printer, convenience store clerk, security guard, adult bookstore clerk, and cab driver. As a cab driver, he drove all areas of Sacramento. He lasted longer at jobs that had the least amount of personal interaction with his employer. Security guard and cab driver positions were the longest jobs he held. I lost track of how many jobs he worked over the years.

Our refrigerator contained a melted stick of butter, a pitcher of Kool-Aid, and three pieces of dried-up bologna because someone didn't close the package right. Our pockets were empty, we were hungry, and the electric bill was due.

THE DARKEST NIGHT

IT WAS A DREARY LOOKING MORNING OUTSIDE AND INSIDE OUR APARTMENT. THE walls were yellowed from years of cigarette smoke. The light bulbs were low wattage and barely lit the rooms. Our front apartment window faced north so very little sun snuck through to share its light. You had to walk outside in order to soak up any Vitamin D if you lived in The Blue Apartments.

I looked forward to leaving the apartment to greet the sun, so I slipped on my short little tropical colored dress with matching dress panties to apply for a job. The dress was trendy, a horrible one at that. It wasn't much longer than a tennis skirt and came with matching panties. Bend over too far and the mystery was over. So, I ended up walking like the girls on the Star Trek television show, my body never bending at the hips.

I strapped my brown leather platform shoes on and hiked ten city blocks to apply for a hostess position on 3rd and J Street downtown. I couldn't believe after all the time I spent filling out the application, the manager didn't even look at it. He hired me on the spot.

"Thank you so much. I appreciate this." I gathered up my papers and stood up to leave.

"Sure. Oh, and our policy is that the servers and the hostess wear dresses while working. Like what you're wearing now." His eyes dropped down to my feet and dragged themselves up to my face.

"Oh, okay, I'll see you tomorrow morning." I walked out of the restaurant happy to be employed.

Ah, yes… times were different in the 70s.

I knew I could keep a job. I was used to people telling me what to do. A full meal a day drew me back to restaurant work. Between customers, if I wasn't organizing around the cash register, I was studying the menu to decide what I would order for lunch. Employees got one free meal during their shift. I usually only ate one meal a day, so I wanted to be sure I relished every single bite of what I had.

Yogi got hired at the same restaurant not long after I did. He stayed in the back, washing dishes and flirting with every server that walked by. He was needy for anyone's attention, male or female. It seemed all the smiles, laughs, and positive vibes in the world couldn't raise his self-confidence. Yogi established his self-worth early on and it seemed nothing was going to change it.

Of course, it wasn't long before he lost this job. "That's it. I've had it up to here!" was one of Yogi's overused expressions. He said it every time he had enough of his employer's "abuse." Yogi couldn't take any more of what this manager was dishing out. Someone mistreated Yogi again and right under my nose too. I didn't hear a thing or even see it coming. Still, I always trusted the stories he laid out for me.

A large cab company was hiring drivers, so Yogi decided to apply. We were both thrilled when he got hired but even more excited each morning to count his tips and be able to eat that day. After several weeks I was amazed Yogi was still employed. I was so used to him getting fired, I thought something was wrong.

———

AS THE SAYING GOES, "A LEOPARD NEVER CHANGES ITS SPOTS." I have never heard of a reformed serial rapist. Maybe there have been some, and I hope so. Yogi's perversions began at fifteen and a half, if not earlier. Could Yogi rape all those women in Japan and just stop raping with no professional help? It's hard to believe we arrived in Sacramento in 1975, and he waited over a year to rape again, unless he was raping women when we first arrived. It's possible the crimes weren't public information, or the police pinned them on another rapist. There were plenty to choose from. There was a rapist loose who committed over forty rapes the previous year the East Area Rapist attacks began. No one was charged for the crimes. Today, there is hardly a mention of that rapist anywhere online.

While we both fumbled through each day just trying to make it, something horrible and wicked was about to begin that would change so many lives in Sacramento and surrounding towns. A serial rapist would hold several cities hostage for years by pure fear alone. He would baffle law enforcement for over forty years. Worst of all, he robbed each woman and their families of their security, trust, and hope. He was called the East Area Rapist.

The East Area Rapist committed his first ten rapes during the last six months of 1976, which I was oblivious to. I wandered the downtown streets of Sacramento along with Yogi without a clue or care in the world about my safety. We didn't own a television and were too broke to get the newspaper, so I was unaware of what happened in our community. Police kept the first seven attacks from the media because they didn't want to alarm the public.

It was the darkest night for a twenty-three-year-old woman who lived in Rancho Cordova. Her father took a flight to Boston for six weeks to visit relatives. The EAR broke into her home, bound her, and raped her. He only stayed in the home for about twenty minutes and was gone.

The young woman's description of the rapist matched Yogi. As I delved into the attacks, I would later find that Yogi's physical description matched many of the rapes committed by the EAR. Yogi's hair was thick and dark, and his arms and legs were covered in dark hair. He was 5 ft. 10 inches and weighed between 160 and 170 lbs. His build was muscular and thin, exactly how the young woman described her rapist.

In hindsight, I wonder if Yogi gave the father a cab ride to the airport. Did he see the daughter say goodbye to her dad before he drove off? Since Yogi grew up in Massachusetts and was familiar with Boston, the father and he would have a lot in common to talk about. A week went by after her father left, then the girl began to receive hang-up calls. Was the rapist learning her schedule? The rapist attacked right before her father returned. Was the rapist waiting to give the victim time to forget what he looked like? These questions ran through my mind when I began to read about the East Area Rapist decades after the crimes.

She told the police that the rapist was in his early twenties. Yogi was twenty-four-years old in 1976. Joseph DeAngelo was thirty-one-years old in 1976. If Joseph DeAngelo raped this young woman in Rancho Cordova, it would have taken him about three and a half hours to get there and three and a half hours to return home. At the time this rape occurred, he worked full time as a police officer in Exeter, California.

PLAY WITH IT

WE FINISHED PLAYING A GAME OF CHESS AND POLISHED OFF A pitcher of strawberry Kool-Aid. From experience I knew my tongue was red, but I stuck it out of my mouth and asked Yogi if it was. It was my inexperienced way of seducing him. It seemed to work. He poked his red tongue out too, and before long we were both naked and tangled up like a pretzel on our sofa.

Out of nowhere, Yogi slapped my butt hard three or four times. Stunned, I removed myself from him and stood up.

"What the hell was that?"

"Oh, I thought you might like it."

"Might like it? Might like it? What makes you think I would like that? Have you not listened to a word I have said? I spent years getting beat with a board and had to watch others get beat." Before I realized what my arms were doing, I slapped his face, his arms, his head, and anything part of him.

"Like it? There, like it? There's some real love for you. Hope you like it." Yogi lay there with his shriveled penis, blocking my slaps. Fury flooded my veins. It was time for one of Yogi's nightly strolls through the neighborhood, so he got dressed and left. I dragged my seething body to bed.

In Carmichael, about eight miles from the first East Area Rapist attack, a 16-year-old girl and her 15-year-old sister woke up to the East Area Rapist one Saturday night while their parents were away for a few days. This attack marks the first time the rapist lubricated his penis with lotion and ordered the victim to play with it after he bound her wrists behind her back. He leaned over, got close to her ear, and asked the young teen, "Have you ever fucked before?"

The girls' description of the rapist and what he did sounded like Yogi again. White, in his 20s, muscular and about 5'10". I remembered when Yogi straddled me from behind and wanted me to "play with it," and I can still hear his voice whispering in my ear, "Do you like to fuck?"

"No, thirteen-year-old girls don't do this!" was my response to him in Atlanta. The memory of me correcting him from "Do you like to fuck?" to "Have you ever fucked?" makes me want to vomit.

I searched each of the youngest girls in all of the attacks and found the East Area Rapist asked the younger victims, "Have you ever fucked before?" He asked the older victims, "Do you like to fuck?"

What the hell, Yogi? I really wanted to be wrong about this, but everything began to point to Yogi. Even after forty years I didn't love him or even like him anymore, but I sure didn't want to know he hurt so many people.

I asked my present husband if this was considered normal sexual behavior. He told me the odds of several men acting out the same role playing and using the exact words is compelling. Especially playing such a deviant role. The more I read, the more I realized that Yogi committed many of the East Area Rapist crimes.

I buried Yogi's past so deep inside and so long ago. All the memories of our sex life... well, I buried those as well. But then they all emerged like weeds erupting from the ground and then I remembered. Things he did and said, places we lived, and the jobs he held seemed like missing puzzle pieces that fit.

We both missed living in Bakersfield. The town rolled up by six in the evening, but it still was a great place to walk around and window shop. Sometimes Yogi and I would be the only two people walking around. We might hear a car driving in the distance or pass by a bar and hear the clinking of drinking glasses or someone leaving.

We would walk back to the Padre Hotel and get settled in for the night only to have Yogi want to go out again. I opted for my beauty sleep; but the night seemed to call out to him, and he would be gone every single night.

When the East Area Rapist surprised the fourth young woman in her driveway, he forced her to the side of her parent's home. He told her, "All I want is money to get to Bakersfield." He pushed her inside the home, tied and gagged her. There she lay while he rummaged through the house and made himself at home with their food. He forced her to masturbate him as he straddled her from behind.

After raping her, the EAR dragged her outside and tied her to a post on the patio. He left behind two empty Coors beer cans in their kitchen, then stole her car to make his escape.

Law enforcement believed that the EAR's comment about getting to Bakersfield was a ploy to throw off investigators. I'm thinking maybe he wanted to return to Bakersfield, to live a simple life in a town that made him feel he was a part of it.

The EAR helped himself to everyone's food in the majority of all the attacks. He rummaged through their refrigerator and cupboards as if they were his own. It not only reminds me how Yogi got his nickname in the service, but the fact he was always hungry. Sometimes after eating a meal at home, he rifled through cupboards looking for more food.

It was just the beginning for the East Area Rapist, but law enforcement didn't see a serial rapist in the works just yet. He was hovering right under their radar.

"Y" IS FOR YOGI

STROLLING THROUGH CAPITAL PARK, WATCHING THE SQUIRRELS DART through the trees, I asked Yogi, "How come you still go by the name Yogi even though you're out of the Marine Corps?"

"I like the nickname. I don't identify with my given name. I'm not that person anymore."

I wondered if he thought by changing his name, he changed his life. He ruined his given name, so he clung to the name his Marine buddies gave him. Many years later, around the year 2000, he renamed himself, "Liam." The name, Liam, is of Irish descent and means a strong-willed warrior. I'm not so sure he ever won any of the inner battles he fought. Back in the day I hoped Yogi turned a new leaf and started his life over. It was fine with me, so I continued to call him Yogi.

"No matter how many times a snake sheds its skin, it will always be a snake." –Author unknown

———

A YOUNG WOMAN WAS SNUGGLED IN BED with her three-year-old son one Tuesday morning after her husband left for work. How warm and safe they must have felt. It was about 6:45 a.m. when there was a noise in the house. Before the woman had time to react, a stranger was at her bedroom door. She screamed, and he ordered her to shut up. He told her he wouldn't hurt her if she cooperated with him.

The East Area Rapist held a knife to the woman's throat and bound her so tight her hands turned black. I can only imagine the fear running through the veins of the mother as she lay there helpless.

As mother and son lay tied up in her bed, the intruder scoured the house looking for money. His fingers pawed through her underwear drawer. When the masked man returned to check on them, he ran his sharp serrated knife along her body, then left the room again. He dragged a chair to the front door, then returned to the bedroom and told the woman he found some money and he would leave soon.

Money wasn't the only thing he came for. The young woman heard him ripping cloth. He followed his usual M.O. with the lotion, then raped her. He told her, "Do it like you do with the captain. You looked good at the Officers Club." He told her he saw her at a dance with the captain. She told police saying these things aroused him and he climaxed. He repeated his lotion routine then returned to the kitchen to prepare something to eat, then left.

Police arrived with their bloodhounds. The dogs followed the rapist's scent over her fence and stopped at a curb near a neighborhood of new homes. Law enforcement believed the rapist parked his car in that spot.

The woman described the rapist as a white male, about 5'9" or 5'10" tall, and of medium weight. She reported to the police that his penis was small.

A few days prior to this attack, a neighbor saw a suspicious man standing near another neighbor's home staring at the woman. He was a white male, about 5'10" and weighed about 170 lbs. He had thick dark hair. When he noticed the neighbor looking at him, he walked back to his dark green car and drove off. This is the same spot the bloodhounds led the police to after the rape.

Everything from lengthy stalking to entering the home, shoelaces used for ligatures, masturbating himself, rummaging, eating the victim's food, and escaping through fields and canals, all set the East Area Rapist's preferred method of operation.

There are a few things about this attack that took my breath away.

1. Yogi often borrowed Betty's boyfriend's green car.
2. Yogi's physical description matches the rapist.
3. The rapist spent time going through the victim's underwear drawer. Yogi had an underwear fetish.
4. Setting a chair in front of the front door is what my mother used to do when my father was out of town. I also used this method when Yogi worked late nights.
5. The rapist forced the victim to play with his penis with her hands tied behind her back, the same way he had done with me while role playing.
6. The rapist dragged a knife across her stomach. He carried out this frightening deed in this attack and a few others.

Investigators believed the EAR used 'red herrings' to throw them off track. When the rapist spoke of the McClellan Air Force Base Officers Club, police thought this was another red herring. The references to the officer's club and seeing her at a dance with the captain make me think of Yogi and his role-playing during sex. Yogi despised authority, especially military authority. In his mind, taking the wife of a captain would have been an achievement to him. He would have reveled in that thought. Maybe that is why he climaxed when he asked her if "his dick was like the captain's." It aroused him to talk dirty.

Law enforcement used bloodhounds to track the suspect. When the dogs were given the scent to follow, they slobbered profusely and went crazy. Some handlers say tracking dogs will behave this way when the scent is of a person on drugs. Is it possible the bloodhounds reacted to the scent of marijuana? Yogi surely smelled of that. The chances of DeAngelo taking drugs while working as a police officer seem slim. I read that DeAngelo had always been a non-smoker. At several different attacks cigarette butts were found, usually where they believe the EAR lay in wait. In some attacks, the EAR smelled like cigarette smoke. At a couple of the attacks the EAR smoked a cigarette or stole a pack. Would the rapist go to this much trouble to set up a red herring? This was a rapist who smoked.

———

A ten-year-old boy woke to his small dog barking in the garage. When he let it out the sliding door his eyes met with a half-naked masked stranger standing in his yard. The kitchen screen was off the window. The boy slammed the door, locked it, and ran to his mothers' bedroom. Meanwhile, the intruder climbed in through the kitchen window.

The mother woke to her breathless son telling her there was a man coming through the kitchen window. She called the Operator, but no one answered. She tried to reach her neighbor, but they didn't answer either. I can only imagine how fast her heart was beating when no one answered her frantic pleas for help.

It was too late. The stranger opened her door and the two became his seventh victims. After he tied them up, he rummaged through the home and searched for food. When he returned to her, he said only inches from her face, "You're beautiful."

"Please don't hurt me. I'm pregnant." He gagged and blindfolded her. Once he untied her legs, he marched her back to her bedroom to search through her dresser drawers. He brought her back to the family room where he removed her clothing. "You have a beautiful body. Do you lay out in the sun?" She nodded yes because the gag was still in her mouth. The woman felt his gloveless hands fondling her body. He violated her, then left the room to finish going through the kitchen drawers.

"You lied. You said there was no more money. I'm going to kill you for lying. There was more money inside the desk." His sharp knife taunted her from her cheeks to her torso, slowly and lightly on her body. He traced a "Y" on her body, then moved the blade along her neck as if it mimicked a throat slitting. He followed his usual M.O. with his lotion, then raped her.

The mother used a little psychology on him. "You're such a good lover," she tells him. The rapist stops to reply, "No one ever said that before. Most people just laugh at me." She then asks, "Do you like to be complimented?"

"Yes. People make fun of me, especially since something happened to my face." He rose to check the clock in the kitchen, looked through a few drawers and checked inside the refrigerator for food. The mother listened to him eating in her kitchen.

There was a large open field behind her home, slated for a housing development. A car started up after the rapist left the house. It sounded like a large American car driving from that field. Her neighbor told the police she heard the same thing. Another neighbor saw headlights from a car in the field five hours before the attack.

Law Enforcement brought in the bloodhounds to trace the rapist's steps. They stopped at the center of the field where the mother and neighbor noted that a car left. From the tire tracks, they figured it was a large American car that was parked behind the home.

The mother and son described the rapist as medium built, about 5'7" with dark hair on his arms and legs. The mother's son told police, "He had big blue eyes."

Joseph DeAngelo is light-haired with light blue eyes. Was the ten-year-old boy describing Yogi's big striking blue eyes that night? Did they describe Yogi's dark brown leg and arm hair?

Is it possible the large American-made car was a Dodge Coronet or a Ford? Back in the 70s, the cab companies used large American-made cars for their cabs. They definitely had loud motors.

In the 80s I read, "How to Win Friends and Influence People" by Dale Carnegie. I wanted to try out what I learned from the book on Yogi. I expected he would laugh at me and that would be that. He did the laundry earlier and stood at the end of our bed, folding it. Stacks of clean clothes laid over the top of the bed. I looked into his eyes and said, "You know, you are so great at doing our laundry. Better than me! You're the best at it."

"Really? You think so?"

"Yep."

By his reaction, you would think I just complimented him on some remarkable ability! Our conversation stunned me, and I ran to finish the book because what I read worked. It surprised me he didn't see right through me and my test. He was an incredible manipulator, but easily manipulated himself. The EAR's reply to the victim who told him he was "such a good lover" is just how Yogi would have reacted in the situation.

Kids can be the most heartless of all sometimes. Yogi's hormones hit his teen years with a vengeance. Acne ravaged his face. It not only embarrassed him but shredded any confidence he had. Everyone laughed at him in school, the boys *and* the girls. Strangers would give him advice on how to get rid of it. His parents accused him of never washing his face and provoked him as much as his classmates. By the expression on Yogi's face, and the inflection in his voice when he told me his story, I got the message that his acne problem was serious.

The rapist placed a blanket over the mother when she said she was cold. Yogi would wreak havoc, experience a moment of guilt, and believe he fixed everything by some small considerate gesture. His personality bleeds right into the descriptions of each rape. Again, he traced the letter "Y" on the woman with a knife.

Detective Richard Shelby, who is retired from the Sacramento County Sheriff's Department, was one of the first involved in the East Area Rapist case. He wrote in his book, *Hunting A Psychopath*, that he thought it might have represented an incision used in autopsies.

But in an autopsy, the deceased is cut from the top of both shoulders to the lower part of the breastbone. The incision then goes straight to the pubic bone. Investigators didn't suspect that the rapist's first name began with a "Y." "Y" is for Yogi. Was this act Yogi's way of branding her?

Police and media kept the first seven attacks by the East Area Rapist concealed. At this point, law enforcement was aware they had a serial rapist on their hands.

The East Area Rapist spent no more than a half hour during attack #8. Attack # 7 occurred about eighteen hours earlier. He chose not to rape the eighth victim for unknown reasons. He left the house in her car. This wasn't the first time he stole a victim's car. It may have allowed him to escape faster, avoid police and tracking dogs, or get back to his vehicle quicker.

Finally, the news broke to the public after attack #8. "Man Hunted as Suspect in 8 Rapes," read the headline in the Sacramento Bee Newspaper. Warren Holloway, a Bee staff writer, authored the article on November 4, 1976. Detective Shelby described the suspect as "White, has a pale complexion, maybe between 5 ft. 8 in. – 6 feet tall, of a medium build, 25 to 35 years old, and has dark hair which hangs over his ears to his collar."

In 1976, Joseph DeAngelo worked as a police officer in Exeter, California. In the 70s, police officers wore their hair short. Of the photos I have seen of DeAngelo during this time, his hair was short. Yogi's length of hair varied depending on whether he had money to get a haircut or not. Detective Shelby's description seemed to be a closer match to Yogi.

GOMEN-NASAI
(I AM SORRY)

EVERY BIRTHDAY WE WERE "TOO BROKE TO EVEN PAY ATTENTION," YOGI would say. I can't remember ever giving each other presents to commemorate our day. Even cards cost too much. We made our own birthday cards from notebook paper. The cost of a card was almost the same as a pack of cigarettes. We had our priorities, as asinine as they were. But we always made promises to each other that the next birthday would be better.

"Gomen-nasai," he would say in Japanese (as if he didn't know how to say "I'm sorry" in English), "Next year we'll buy new clothes, and both get dressed up. I'll show up in my cab and take you to the finest restaurant in Sacramento. We can do whatever your heart desires." Deep down inside I always knew that was crap, a few piles high, but pretended to accept the lie, anyway. I started telling him the same thing every year.

In November 1976, I turned 21 years old. I was officially old enough to drink alcohol in California. It didn't seem as exciting since the drinking age was 18 in Georgia and Massachusetts. I had already seen enough bars. Yogi mentioned we should celebrate my 21st birthday in one of the neighborhood bars.

I held the utility bills in my hand and fanned my face as I stared deep inside the empty refrigerator. I glanced back at Yogi with my eyebrows perched high.

"We can go some other night. Let's just stay home."

"No, it's your 21st birthday. You can't stay home. Trust me, we won't have to pay for a single drink."

He wouldn't take no for an answer.

"How many times do you turn 21?"

I realized he wasn't going to drop it until I said yes. I only hoped he didn't plan to drink and dash.

The neighborhood dive bar took just a few minutes to get to from our apartment. That evening the 'Torch Club' was loosely packed with old guys and a few women. There was that heavy whiskey smell again, belting me in the face the minute we walked in. Our eyes patrolled the entire bar in a matter of seconds before we climbed on to the heavy black leather stools at the end. Yogi taught me to always give a room the 'once over' before choosing a place to sit. If you choose the wrong spot, it is harder to move after you sit down.

Rubbing a glass with a towel, the older bartender sauntered over. "What shall it be?"

"The young lady would like a Sloe Gin Fizz and I will take a Coors. She turned 21 today." He said it with an enthusiastic smile and slight gleam in his eye.

After the bartender glanced at me twice, he said, "Well, happy birthday to you little lady. Your drinks are on the house!"

It seemed all the old fellas raised their glasses in unison and wished me the happiest birthday.

One of them peered at me with his watery eyes. "I remember 21," he said, as his voice faded. His freckled fingers looked like sausages grasping at his short glass. He held his drink up in the air then tilted his head back, finishing the amber liquid. He then told the bartender to bring us another round. The rest of the guys followed suit, buying our drinks all night long.

Yogi and I drank for hours but didn't spend a dime of our money. That was a good thing since we only had about that much in our pockets. We listened to the old guys' stories, laughed at their dirty jokes, and then eventually stumbled home. It turned out to be a night to remember.

———

ON NOVEMBER 10, 1976, JUST FOUR DAYS BEFORE MY 21st BIRTHDAY, the East Area Rapist attacked a sixteen-year-old girl. This attack became number nine. She was home alone when the rapist busted into her home. She tried to scream, but he held a sharp knife to her throat.

"Shut up or I'll kill you. All I want is your money," he told her with his smelly breath. He tied her hands behind her back and led her to the backyard. He left her there and returned to inside the house, making sure nothing was out of place, as if there was no struggle. Once back outside, he asked again. "Where's your money?" The young girl told him she didn't have any.

"Damn, no money? Ah, man, no money?" he asked. The victim said that he sounded very desperate and truly disappointed.

"Do you like to fuck?"

The teen did not respond. The rapist forced the young girl from her yard, guiding and sort of dragging her toward a canal behind her street. He sat her down by a tree and cut her jeans off with his knife. His plan unraveled as her leg got loose.

"This isn't working right," he said. He asked her a few questions about where he might know her.

"Do you go to American River College?"

She told him she went to San Juan High School and gave him a fake name. He called her a liar.

Then he became nervous. "I have to wait for my parents to leave. I'm going to take off in my car," he mumbled. This attack was considered a failure.

It's likely he meant this attack for the teen's next-door neighbor who attended American River College. I wonder if that's why he asked the sixteen-year-old victim if she liked to fuck instead of, "Have you ever fucked before?" The neighbor girl was college age. The East Area Rapist made a few mistakes like this during his reign of terror, but not many.

The young teenage girl told police he was a white male between eighteen and twenty-three years old, about 165 pounds, standing around 5 foot 10 inches. He wore military fatigues, a military fatigue jacket, and black square-toed shoes. He also wore a leather hood with slits cut out for the eyes and mouth. His leg and head hair were brown.

Was Yogi so disappointed that the young girl didn't have any money because he couldn't buy a birthday present for me? It was four days before my 21st birthday, he knew it was a big deal.

I can't imagine DeAngelo, a thirty-one-year-old full-time police officer, husband, and father, who lived several miles away, find the time necessary to commit these crimes. The time needed to study the habits of each victim and their families alone would take a considerable amount of time. Yogi's access to personal and professional addresses came with the job. A person can learn a lot about the comings and goings of an individual by where they are picked up and dropped off.

The EAR attacked in different areas of town. Time spent to commit each crime also adds up. The East Area Rapist sometimes spent two to three hours inside each home. Now in hindsight, knowing what I do about Yogi, it is easy for me to see what he was doing. I can see a graveyard shift person, a twenty-four-year-old cab driver or security guard living in Sacramento doing those horrible crimes with some time to spare. No one was checking on his time. Not even me. And when I would ask the next morning what time he got home, he always lied, so I stopped asking.

BROKEN KNIVES

AS THE STRANGER WALKED FROM THE SIDEWALK, ONTO HER YARD and through her side gate, her dog raged inside her home. She looked out one of her windows to see what was going on. When she did, she locked eyes with the stranger looking back. He was as startled as she was, and so he ran off.

The woman told police the stranger was a White male, about 175 lbs., and about 5'11" tall. The style of his hair reminded her of the 50s. The sides were short and it was "combed up in front." She was quoted as saying, "His haircut seemed polished, as if he had just left the salon." She also told the police that this guy was agile and looked athletic. He wore a light windbreaker-type jacket, despite the temperature being in the low 40s. Because the stranger left her property, the police wouldn't come out to check anything. There were other sightings of prowlers in the same neighborhood leading up to this attack. It would be the same evening the East Area Rapist committed the 11th attack on Glenville Circle, a street away from La Riviera Drive.

Three hours later, that woman's neighbor woke to a bright light in her face and a knife to her throat. The East Area Rapist tied her up, raped her several times, ate her food, and rifled through all her drawers, cupboards and closets. He spent four long hours in her home, longer than usual. It must have been unbearable for her. She described his penis to be five or six inches long, larger than her husband's penis.

The twenty-five-year-old was the first Asian woman attacked by the EAR. The young woman worked as a secretary at the State Capital building. Before the rapist left the home, he brought the victim's knives into the living room and broke off all the blades. This was the only attack that the EAR did this. My first thought for him doing this was to keep the young woman from attempting suicide after he left. I can't think of another reason for him doing that. Did she say something to him that would make him think she considered it? Did Yogi flashback to the crimes he committed in Japan? He knew the language. Did they exchange words?

Yogi was a history buff and was consumed by learning about other cultures. I don't have all the details to this attack so I can only theorize what went on in his mind that night. Was he lost in thought about the ancient Jigai Ritual? It is a ritual suicide by women who were disgraced by rape and feared the social stigma placed upon them. Even though it was a ritual practiced long ago, Yogi had the tendency to fall into role playing when certain circumstances suited him. This may have been one of those times.

The East Area Rapist stole the victim's car and drove it about a mile and a half from her home. He parked it in front of an apartment complex.

The description of the prowler's hairstyle reminds me of how Yogi styled his hair every now and then, combed back with a bump in front.

The public grew more concerned about their safety. Law enforcement formed an East Area Rapist task force after Attack #11. The media began to shed more light on this serial rapist who lurked about Sacramento.

On January 22, 1977, two days before Attack #12, a neighbor watched a man walk across her neighbor's yards. He slithered around bushes and hedges and hoped to be invisible. The neighbor tried to observe where he was traveling. He ended up twenty feet in front of her. They stared at one another. When she saw his face, he stood there, not saying a word. The frightened neighbor turned around to go back inside her house and the man disappeared.

The neighbor described the stranger to be a White male, about six feet tall, with curly brown hair. I haven't been able to muster any photos of DeAngelo with brown curly hair, but Yogi's hair was brown and curly, and sometimes described as wavy.

He wore a brown jacket and dark pants. On January 27, 1977, three days after the attack, the same neighbor found Marlboro cigarette butts outside on the ground in front of her living room window. Yogi's brand.

It was a Monday morning about 1:00 a.m. on January 24, 1977, in the city of Citrus Heights. A young 25-year-old woman, woke to an intruder grabbing her, blindfolding her, and binding her arms together. She could smell his strong body odor. He left her lying there, scared to move while he rummaged through her home, then returned to rape her. An ice pick was his weapon of choice that evening, and he threatened to jam it into her neck several times. As he lubricated his penis with lotion, he made her guess what he was doing. Then he raped her again.

The rapist drank two beers he brought with him and left the cans behind. He foraged through her refrigerator, took a big bite from a block of cheese, and left it on her counter. He terrorized this woman for two hours before leaving.

The rapist left footprints resembling waffle stomper boots in the neighbor's yard. Police dogs tracked him two blocks from the victim's home where he had parked. This was a new area for him. The woman described his penis as small, four or five inches. She told police the rapist seemed more interested in scaring her than raping her.

I remember when Yogi would kiss me awake just to see the startled look on my face when we lived in Atlanta.

We celebrated Yogi's 25th birthday on January 24, 1977. When I read the East Area Rapist attacked the twenty-five-year-old woman on this date, it repulsed me. His feeling of entitlement on his birthday. Out of 365 days, one of the EAR's rapes reported occurred on Yogi's birthday.

The young victim noticed his body odor. A few other women attacked by the EAR mentioned his strong body odor, as well. When Yogi sweat, it quickly caused a strong pungent odor. He would sweat after walks, sex, if it was too hot in the house, and after any exercise. He never wanted the heater on, even in the winter months. In several EAR cases, he turned off the heat to the house, even in the wintertime. The reason he might have done this was to hear outside noises better or to eliminate the odor from his profuse sweating, or both.

Growing up in Massachusetts and living in Japan acclimated Yogi to cold weather. He always dressed in lighter clothing, even during the winter months in Sacramento. Yogi said if there wasn't snow on the ground, it wasn't winter yet.

Smoking Marlboro's and drinking Coors were Yogi's favorite pastimes. It is unfortunate law enforcement didn't make any castings of the large bite mark in the block of cheese. Yogi had a distinctive bite. He had a noticeable space between his top front teeth. I used to tease him and say, "You part your hair on the side, and you part your teeth in the middle."

Prior to Attack #13, nearby neighbors taking a walk witnessed three police cars drive by with their flashing lights on. As they did, a masked man came from behind a bush and onto the sidewalk. He stood there watching the cars go by with his hands on his hips. The couple walked past him and neither paid any attention to the other. It sounds like such a small thing, but everyone has a normal stance. Yogi's stance was standing with his hands on his hips; something he almost always did when he was just standing, waiting in line, or waiting on something.

A neighbor who lived close by witnessed an unfamiliar man walking toward the home of Attack #13, only a few minutes before the rape. The stranger was a young White man in his early twenties, thin build, and about 5' 11." His hair was collar length, and he had a mustache.

The East Area Rapist entered the young woman's home after her husband left for work. He began to restrain her and tie her up. When she tried to break free, she felt a gun in his right pocket and worked it out into the open. She almost pulled the trigger but changed her mind. The thought of her sleeping daughter in the other room getting hurt made her think twice. The rapist made her pay for that by hitting her several times.

The East Area Rapist ran his knife along her stomach, mimicking the same letter "Y" behavior he did with the other attack.

The woman described the rapist as a white male about 5 foot 11 inches, with hairy legs. He weighed about 185 lbs. He left his cigarette butts in their ashtray.

If the woman felt the rapist's gun in his right pocket, chances are he was right-handed. Yogi is right-handed; DeAngelo is left-handed.

It was after 8:00 a.m. when the masked man left. There were many sightings of him by neighbors and a teacher saw a man running in a park area nearby. On a trail by the school police found empty beer cans, Marlboro cigarette butts, and tennis shoe prints.

Investigators found a sample of blood that didn't belong to the family. The woman's blood was type B. They tested the sample, and it turned out to be 'A positive'.

The East area Rapist also left his calling card on the picnic table at Attack #10. A bloodied Band-Aid was found by investigators. It didn't belong to anyone else in the household. The lab checked it out and determined the blood on the Band-Aid was 'A positive'.

Investigators found blood samples at Attacks #10, 13, and 14. They lost Attack #14's sample before obtaining results. Attacks #10 and #13 resulted in blood type A+. Law enforcement retrieved saliva from a spoon at Attack #16. All the blood samples and all the evidence were discarded many years ago, so none can be tested today.

Yogi had a Marine Corps ID card that had blood type A+ listed on it. One in three people have blood type A+. Law enforcement stated the

EAR is a non-secretor. Eighty percent of Caucasians are secretors and 20% are non-secretors. A secretor secretes his blood type antigens into his body fluids like saliva, mucus in their digestive tract, semen, etc. A non-secretor doesn't secrete or secretes very little. I have no knowledge whether Yogi or Joseph DeAngelo are non-secretors, but they both have blood type 'A positive'.

RIPON COURT SHOOTING

A PROWLER WAS ON THE LOOSE ON RIPON COURT IN SACRAMENTO while Raymond Miller and his son, Rodney, were home. About 10:30 p.m., Rodney came in from the garage when he and his father heard a noise in their backyard. They both went to investigate and discovered a man's shadow near a bush. The prowler ran from the backyard and jumped over the fence into the neighbor's yard. Rodney scaled the fence and chased after him.

The prowler stopped in the driveway to contemplate his next move. Rodney got a good look at him. He was a White male, about twenty years old, close to 5'10" and about 170 lbs. The homeowner's son bolted toward him, and the stealthy man ran to the fence and jumped over it. Rodney grabbed his leg, which caused the prowler to fall on the ground on the other side of the fence. There he lay in a crouched position. Rodney made it halfway over the fence when the prowler pulled out a gun with his left hand and shot him in the stomach. The criminal got away and Rodney was raced to a nearby hospital. He survived, but it left him with a lifetime of health issues. The prowler never returned. Rodney almost caught him that winter night.

Law enforcement is confident the East Area Rapist fired those bullets into Rodney Miller's stomach that evening. He used a 9mm weapon. The same weapon may have been used to threaten previous rape victims. This area fit his usual MO. He preferred striking victims who lived near levees, schools, and canals. This aided him in escaping with quickness and ease. Ripon Court was close to a school, and the Miller's home backed up to the second house from the corner.

Law Enforcement made a composite for this crime, and they gave it the nickname, "Ripon Court Shooter." Others have referred to the composite as the Suspicious Male Model, and Ripon Court Prowler. In 2016, the FBI used this composite in promoting the public to recall any information to aid in their hunt for the East Area Rapist. This composite is one of only three used for that purpose. Rodney Miller aided in this composite, along with four women who noticed a suspicious man walking in the area that evening.

———

When my eyes first met with the eyes of the Ripon Court Shooter composite, I whispered under my breath, "Oh no, Yogi, what have you done?" Despite the shooter using his left hand to fire at Rodney, I am convinced it was Yogi. I desperately wanted to be wrong. I compared the composite to a 1981 photo of Yogi. Although in the 1981 photo he has a mustache, the full lips of the prowler are a carbon copy of Yogi's lips. The other features resemble Yogi as well. Joseph DeAngelo has zero similarities to this composite. I am certain it was Yogi in the Miller's backyard that evening.

HAIRY PERP WITH DARK BLUE EYES

PRIOR TO ATTACK # 14, NEIGHBORS FOUND A CLOTH BAG STUFFED IN A BUSH in front of their home. Curious, they looked inside and found a flashlight, gloves, and a ski mask. Sensing something wasn't right, they phoned the police to report what they found. Someone answering calls at the police station advised them to throw it all away. *Are you kidding me?* A serial rapist was loose in Sacramento and thirteen women had been viciously violated by him. That's just bad advice even on a perfect day. The family kept the flashlight and tossed the rest. Later, police analyzed the flashlight, but couldn't find any fingerprints.

In the spring of 1977, a 16-year-old girl became the 15th person to be attacked by the East Area Rapist. He brought an ax with him to coerce the young teen to do as he said. That night the EAR wore a balaclava-type mask where it can be pulled down to expose the face. The open face mask allowed her to see his full face. She described it as young and round, and he had wide eyes and a wide mouth. The rapist told her he had an "eight-inch dick," even though the teen described it to resemble the size of a hot dog.

When I was in kindergarten, I was the first to draw the number eight without using two circles on top of one another. My teacher and classmates were thrilled, and I loved every second of those accolades so much, it has been my favorite number my entire life. Yogi joked about everything. He described to me what he would do with his "eight-inch dick." It seemed hilarious because it was my favorite number, but we both knew it wasn't even close to eight inches. I know, I know, it sounds ridiculous, but I easily laughed at everything then. It really is a million little things that put this puzzle together for me.

"Don't make any moves. Lay still or I'll kill you like I did the people in Bakersfield," he said, threatening the couple he just woke up with a bright flashlight. The small family returned earlier in the evening from the drive-in movies. They all went to sleep after arriving to their safe home in Orangevale. And there he was, the East Area Rapist, hiding behind a white mask ready to terrorize the first couple he had ever attacked.

There were a few firsts in Attack # 16. After tying up the couple, he placed cups and saucers on their backs. He used the dishes as an alarm. If either of them moved, the dishes would alert him while he rummaged around the home looking for money.

The EAR left for a moment and walked into the garage. When he returned he wasn't wearing any pants. After removing the dishes from the frightened woman's back, he untied her feet and sat on her hands while he maneuvered his penis between them.

The rapist made himself at home to the family's food. Before raping the young woman in the kitchen, he placed her high heels on her feet. He lifted the woman up onto his lap and while sitting on her kitchen chair raped her again. When he finished, he threw her down on the floor and re-tied her ankles.

The family's small poodle remained quiet during the entire attack. This led officers to believe the rapist stalked the victim, the house, and made friends with the dog in prior days or weeks. The rapist had a slight German accent. The woman described him to be White, about 5'9" with muscular thighs that felt like stubble as if they had been shaved.

Stacking dishes on backs, a slight accent, masturbation, muscular, stubby thigh hair... all point to Yogi. Was Bakersfield on his mind again that night?

A few weeks before this attack, a neighbor saw who she thought was a police officer on the victim's property late one evening. There was no report of this happening. Is it possible she mistook a security guard for a police officer? Yogi had been employed by several different security companies when he wasn't driving a taxicab.

By April 1977, Detective Richard Shelby concluded that two perpetrators existed. Attack #16 in Orangevale and Attack #17 in Carmichael described two different people. Shelby described the rapist in Attack #16, "The hairy perp had dark blue eyes." He had large thighs and abrasive hair, as if he shaved them. His penis was about five inches long and he had a hairy backside. He spoke with a mild German accent. Thirteen days later, in Carmichael, Attack #17 occurred. The M.O. simulated Attack #16, but she described the attacker as a man about 5 ft. 9 inches to 5 ft. 10 inches. His arms and legs had very little hair on them. It was light, and the texture was not coarse. The man in Attack #16 did not match the description of the man in Attack #17, at all.

———

Detective Shelby writes in his book, *Hunting a Psychopath*:

> This assault occurred about the same time I told Lt. Root I could make a case for two suspects in the East Area Rapist series. In a heartbeat Lt. Root responded with, "I don't want to hear about it." He explained, "...

to make that public would create more confusion and panic, in a public which already had a plentiful supply. Go arrest them, then tell me about it," was his response.

———

Detective Richard Shelby couldn't have been any closer to being right. The more descriptions of the East Area Rapist, the clearer it is that there was more than one perpetrator.

I knew the "hairy perp with dark blue eyes."

"I GOT KICKED OUT"

OUR FIRST TELEVISION SET WAS ABOUT AS BIG AS A
POSTAGE STAMP, or so it seemed. Yogi brought it home, plugged it
in and *voilà!* instant happiness for Yogi. He stayed glued to his western
shows, Bruce Lee movies, and Star Trek.

It's the little things that can bring you happiness when you are
struggling. Excitement ran through both of us. One would have thought
we bought our first brand-new car or house. But it was only a tiny television that got three stations. The set was so cheaply made the dial eventually broke off and we had to use a pair of pliers to change the station.

The private school must have conditioned me not to watch it because it was a rare occasion when I did. While news about the East Area
Rapist was plastered on every news station at 5:00 and 11:00 o'clock,
other things kept me occupied and away from the TV. I was never
an avid TV watcher, and the EAR stories were not of interest to me.
Besides, the television found itself in the pawn shop more than in our
apartment. It wasn't until the attacks numbered in the 30s that I found
out about this monster. Mary mentioned it to Yogi and me when we
were visiting one day. At the time, I had no reason to suspect him. Of
course, in hindsight I remember Yogi's reaction to Mary's news: "He
must be good if they haven't caught him yet."

Yogi got a little closer to Betty and her boyfriend. Of course, he had a reason for it. Whatever he did always had an ulterior motive. Betty and her boyfriend owned cars. I paid little attention to which make or model. I just knew Betty's car was white and her boyfriend's car was green. They let Yogi use them from time to time.

When Betty sat in the driver's seat, she controlled every move of that car like a pro. She drove it like she stole it. One Saturday night she took me for a drive. We cruised around J and K Streets downtown. Someone dumped water onto the windshield of her car from the top of a parking garage. The drench of water startled her, and she almost lost control of her car. Betty changed into The Hulk. She regained control and sped around the block and into a parking garage. "Where the heck are we going, Betty?"

"We are going to find the assholes who enjoy trying to kill people." I held on for dear life as she put her foot down on the gas pedal and sped around each corner. Every turn put us on two wheels. When we reached the floor where she found a group of guys, she slammed the car in park. "Betty, Betty, what are you doing?" I screamed. Her door flew open, and she leaned over to grab a tire iron from the back seat floorboard. "Holy shit!" I yelled. "They are going to beat you to death, and I'll be forced to watch it all."

"Okay, motherfuckers, grab your shit, get in your cars and leave or I'm going to bust up every one of you motherfuckers with this tire iron." I almost peed my pants. Their mouths dropped open in disbelief, but every one of them did what she said. She went crazy for a few minutes but accomplished what she wanted. I always felt safe with Betty around.

Betty had Yogi figured out. When I look back now, it's crystal clear. Back then, a smokescreen clouded my vision of the real him. It took me years to see through it all. He manipulated everyone he met. Betty could get him to do anything by complimenting him and building up his confidence. Then she would turn and give me a huge grin. Even though Yogi was a master manipulator; when it came to Betty, he was like a Gumby in a kid's hand.

Betty split up with her boyfriend, and when expenses were too much for her to handle, she moved out. Yogi couldn't have been happier. I'm sure he feared me becoming independent and outspoken, just like her. I was working on that at my own slow pace.

Attack #18 occurred early May 3rd, 1977. It was a Tuesday morning, about 4:30 a.m., a couple woke up to a stranger in their bedroom. He held his flashlight in his left hand and a 45 automatic in his right as he threatened both he would kill them if they moved. Money is what he wanted. At least that's what he told them. He threw shoelaces to the woman and ordered her to tie up her husband. The husband told the rapist his wallet was on the dresser. The intruder wasn't happy about the amount and threatened the couple for more. She told him she had more in her purse. The rapist acted as if he was a drug addict in need of drugs, then he stopped his charade.

The EAR re-tied the husband tighter and marched the woman upstairs to check her purse for more money. He lay the victim on the floor near the bathroom where he placed a shower cap over her face and tied her legs together. He stepped downstairs for a short time. When the rapist returned, he tied her to a table leg and looked around the house. He checked the refrigerator for food.

The victim listened to the EAR putting lotion on himself. "Do you know what this sound is? If you don't tell me, I'll kill you. Bitch! Play with it. Do it like you're doing it to your husband." He then raped her. After he re-tied her, he placed her on her stomach and put glass items on her back.

The EAR returned to the bedroom where the husband lay waiting. After the rapist rummaged through the bedroom closet, he asked the husband if he had been in the service. The husband told him yes; he was in the Air Force. The East Area Rapist told him, "I got thrown out."

The rapist returned to the kitchen to find something to eat. He returned to the bedroom downstairs. With his mouth full of food, he told the husband if he moved, he would hear him and kill everyone in the house.

Police brought tracking dogs to the home after the rapist escaped. The dogs tracked the rapist to the levee behind the victim's home. They found empty beer cans, tire tracks, and shoe prints, but could not connect the items to this crime.

Circumstances of this rape are a little different. The victims lived in a two-story home, as opposed to the usual single-story home. The rapist spoke clearly, instead of speaking in his normal angry whisper. He didn't gag the woman, as he usually did. He took deep breaths at intervals depicting nervousness. Maybe the deep breaths calmed him down. His demeanor wasn't as rough as other rapes in the past. In fact, victims described the calm and gentler demeanor in other rapes.

Some thought the comment, "I got thrown out" was nothing more than a red herring. Experienced liars sprinkle a little truth in with their lies. It makes it more difficult to pick out what is true and what isn't. For me, most of the "red herrings" are puzzle pieces which fit right into the Yogi puzzle. After all, the Marine Corps did throw him out after the horrendous attacks in Japan.

The 21st attack on May 17, 1977, had the normal similarities as most of the attacks. It had some differences, too. He ordered the wife to "Rub me" as opposed to "Play with it." The stranger told the young woman if he heard about this on television, he would go out the next night and kill two people. He told her he had "bunches of televisions."

The woman told police he was about 5 ft. 8 inches to 5 ft. 9 inches, and his penis was about five inches. He had hairy legs and spoke in a youthful voice. He carried his gun in his right hand and a flashlight in his left. The couple said he showed extreme anger toward the husband

and wasn't brutal to the wife. The woman thought the rapist "had an eating obsession." He kept returning to the kitchen to search for food.

It sounds strange that a person would even tell someone he had "bunches of televisions," unless he thought it was something to brag about. Not only was Yogi hungry most of the time, but I was also certain he had an "eating obsession" just like his biological mother.

FOR CRYING OUT LOUD

ONE EVENING I WOKE TO UNFAMILIAR VOICES IN MY LIVING ROOM. Because my head was a little fuzzy from sleep, I listened for a minute to understand what was going on. It sounded like a high-pitched voice talking, squealing, and crying. "Is there a girl crying in my living room?" I wondered. My arm flung the blankets to the side of me, and I tiptoed to my bedroom door. My head peeked around the white door frame and noticed Yogi alone in the living room. Both of his hands were violently scratching each side of his head, as if each hand raced the other. The voice came from Yogi's mouth. The high pitch voice sounded like he was yelling at someone but trying to be quiet about it. His face twisted as he cried. It made him look like he was in pain. I couldn't bear peeking at him any longer. I slowly and quietly walked into the living room, so I wouldn't startle him.

The moment Yogi saw me, he stopped scratching his head and crying.

"What's wrong?" I asked him. It was the first time I witnessed anything like this.

"I'm sorry I woke you up. Sometimes I revisit conversations with my mother. I'll go over a fight and I'll say what I wanted to say to her, but never did. It makes me feel better."

I would understand if someone did this once or twice, but this same bizarre behavior repeated itself for the next fifteen years. His old thoughts whipped up into whirlwinds of head scratching and high-pitched whining. He never shared the details of what his mother and father did to him to push him over the edge.

For many years I woke up to his crazy head scratching and old screaming fights between he and his mother. His actions were odd, to say the least. I encouraged him to get help, but he never did. Years passed and my sweet response to these midnight conversations with himself transformed to impatience and frustration. Eventually, I would bolt out of bed and scream at him, "What the hell, Yogi? Get a grip on yourself! Your mother isn't here and can never hurt you anymore. I have to get up early and go to work."

He always apologized, but the same behavior continued to repeat itself. It never left him. Little by little, Yogi's peculiar habits unveiled themselves.

Strangely enough, the East Area Rapist exhibited similar behavior. It was reported that the attacker cried and said, "It scares my mommy when it's in the news," at the 22nd attack. During Attack #25, the victim told the police that the rapist had a slight accent and he cried while eating in their kitchen. At Attack #26, after raping the woman, he cried and said, "I'm sorry, Ma. Mommy. Please help me. I don't want to do this, Mommy." During Attack #41 he cried, "You Motherfucker. You Motherfucker." He sobbed in a high-pitched voice at several other attacks as well. Most victims believed it was genuine.

———

I used to tell Yogi that he should have been a comedian. "Comedy comes from pain," he would always reply. He had so many shticks tucked in his funny file, which he kept in his head. He did his jokes with many accents, which added to the humor. His accents were in German, Puerto Rican, Spanish, Asian, English, and many others.

Yogi spoke in his normal New England accent. He spoke Japanese well after spending so much time in Japan. Although he didn't stutter, he did so in some of his comic routines.

The East Area Rapist spoke with different accents in many of his attacks. He stuttered during a few attacks. Investigators believed these were just more red herrings. This may be true, or maybe he used different accents to cover up his own New England accent.

———

A NEW APARTMENT BECKONED US TO MOVE FROM THE HELLHOLE on O Street. Yogi brought a newspaper home, and we scoured the apartment rental section. We found one not too far from where we lived. Another nameless apartment building, like O Street. They sold me the minute I stepped into the spacious apartment. The old sofa and chair were a royal blue, a color I'm sure was never fashionable. The chairs looked hideous against the shaggy gold carpet. I didn't find out until later they propped the blue chair up with a block of wood. It didn't matter, we landed in a suitable place. All I knew was the community hallway had a savory smell that made our mouths water. Behind one of those apartment doors lived a fabulous cook. Every evening a new recipe created a wonderful new aroma. Yogi and I drooled, and it became a guessing game to see which one of us figured out what they cooked for dinner.

We lucked out getting another furnished apartment. They attached the bedroom dressers and nightstands to the walls. I suppose they wanted to keep people from stealing them. The two-story, two-bedroom was the last apartment on the left in the back of the building. Stairs turned out to be the best part of the apartment. For several months Yogi had to watch me stand at the bottom of the stairs like Bette Davis, flip my hair to the side and say, "Fasten your seatbelts. It's going to be a bumpy night."

Betty came back to Sacramento for a few days to visit her mom, brother, and me. I barely concealed my delight. I had a sense of pride to be living in a better place than The Blue Apartments. Betty saw our lives change for the better.

We stayed up late, catching up with everything new, and eating every snack we had. Betty brought a bag full of every chip and candy bar you could imagine. I woke up the next morning at my regular time, but let her sleep in. Seemed like she slept forever. I climbed the stairs several times to listen at the guest bedroom door. My ear rested on the hollow-core door. I closed my eyes to help me concentrate and listen better, but nothing. Not even a deep breath or ruffling of the covers.

"Wait a minute, she must be dead. How can she sleep this late? Déjà vu." My throat closed as my stomach bile inched its way up. My blood pounded in my ears. I raced downstairs to the same-looking yellow rotary phone I had nine years ago. I put my index finger in the "O" and let it swirl around when my mom died. History was about to repeat itself for someone else I loved.

I raced back up the stairs, took a deep breath and exploded through the door. Betty's eyes were wide open, and her messy black curls were dancing on her head. She tried to focus on me, "What the hell's the matter?"

Laughing, crying, and coughing, I stammered, "I… I thought you were dead."

"Oh my God, Helen, how the hell do you come up with this shit? You got any coffee?"

An enormous sigh of relief came over me. As I prepared some instant coffee for us, I also wondered how the hell I came up with some of the thoughts I had. It didn't matter because I let the fear go, balanced two full cups of coffee and some toast in my hands, and plodded back up the stairs to enjoy her company.

The front door slammed, and I heard someone running up the carpeted stairs. I didn't realize how late Yogi was returning from work.

He never came home at a set time, even though his shift ended at 6:00 a.m., unless he had to finish driving somewhere or do some paperwork. Betty had things to do that day, so she got up, got dressed, and left. Yogi and Betty looked at each other and raised their eyebrows in unison. I suppose that was their lousy way of saying goodbye to each other.

———

At about 3:45 a.m., the East Area Rapist pried open a bedroom window to a home in Citrus Heights. After climbing in, he woke the sleeping couple with his bright flashlight, and they soon became Attack #20.

"You make a sound and I'll kill you. I have a .45 and I'll kill you if you move. I'm going to take your money and I want some food and then I'll leave in my van." They saw the gun and obeyed the intruder.

The rapist made the wife tie up her husband, then he tied her up. The same routine continued as in the previous rapes. He scoured the house for money. When he found a coffee cup filled with Canadian coins, he shoved it in his coat pocket.

The rapist returned to the bedroom, stacked cups, and saucers on the husband's back, and pushed the wife into the living room. He tied the woman's feet together, took money from her purse and rewarded himself with a beer from the kitchen. After roaming around the home, he returned to the wife with her Vaseline Intensive Care lotion. He covered the television with part of a towel, turned the sound down and forced her to masturbate him.

He stayed in the home for about an hour and a half. The couple told police he had brown collar-length hair, very hairy legs, and no facial hair. He stood about 5 feet, 9 inches to 5 feet, 10 inches. He carried a .45 gun, a sharp knife, and a black zippered gym-type bag. Prior to this rape, the neighborhood experienced a lot of suspicious activity.

On May 13, 1977, about twelve hours before Attack #20, a neighbor on the same street reported a suspicious person. A man sat in his car for two hours. He parked about 6:30 p.m. A neighbor woman thought the police were doing a stakeout. The dark-colored car's paint looked battered, uneven, and peeling. The man sitting in the car wore a rumpled brown uniform. She gave no other description that she could remember. When the man started his car, she noticed his loud engine. It had a loud exhaust.

There was no mistaking the sound of my first car. After I turned the key, it rumbled to life. Thomas cosigned a loan for me, and I bought Betty's brother's car. It was a 1968 Ford Torino with a loud 351 Windsor engine, a Holly carburetor, and a custom paint job. The entire car was black, but the sides appeared whitish with a spider web look. The white portion faded into the black paint. It could be described as "battered, uneven, and peeling."

I barely rested my foot on the gas, and it moved like a jet. There was no way this car could sneak up on anyone. The engine roared from several blocks away.

Betty's brother introduced her to his friend, Thomas. He and Thomas worked the same shift for the same company. It didn't take long before Betty and Thomas were a couple. Yogi and I got along well with Thomas.

I started back to school and took Administration of Justice classes at Sacramento City College. The college wasn't far from our new place on P Street, but we needed a car. I drove it to school for a while but preferred taking the bus because it was too much of a car for me.

Yogi and I lived on P Street when Attack #20 occurred. While at this apartment, Yogi worked as a security guard and taxicab driver. He wore a brown uniform when he worked for a security guard company.

When I read the car's description by the neighbor, I knew it was mine. And the rumpled brown uniform? I knew it was Yogi's.

I started receiving a monthly check from the estate of my parent's retirement benefits... as long as I attended school. So, we graduated from bologna sandwiches to hamburgers and macaroni and cheese. Life was grand. Thomas and Betty's relationship didn't last long. I stayed friends with both for many years. Soon Thomas introduced us to his new girlfriend, Mary. Yogi and I had our doubts when we first heard about her. We didn't know how long the relationship would last, so we remained a little apprehensive. But Mary made it easy for us. In fact, she and I became instant friends and we have remained good friends now for over forty years.

B.K.

THE SUN WAS ALREADY SHINING HOT THROUGH THE KITCHEN WINDOW when Yogi walked through our front door, a little slower than usual. The night before he worked a long shift for the cab company. He complained his entire body hurt, but his shoulder hurt the most. He explained he got into a fight with a fare that didn't pay. The guy tossed Yogi to the ground and his shoulder was hurt. He said he tried to get help at American River Hospital in Carmichael, but they were too busy, and he didn't want to wait. He took it easy and as time went on, his pain subsided.

In May 1977, after terrorizing Victim #22 in south Sacramento, the EAR's quickest escape was scaling a chain link fence in the dark. Law Enforcement think it is likely that the rapist parked on the side of Highway 99 and jumped over a locked gate and onto the ground. The top of the gate had a top bar which made it easier to climb over than the top of the chain link fencing.

Between the highway and chain link fence was a V shaped canal. It would have been easy to climb the gate and jump from the highway side because there was plenty of ground to land on. Jumping from the other side to get back to your car would be dangerous. It would be too difficult to gain your footing with such a small landing space and most likely it would be a full body landing.

Law Enforcement imagines that after jumping to escape after attacking #22, the rapist may have fallen and hurt himself in the canal. Two days after the attack, American River Hospital called police saying a suspicious man resembling the EAR was there with an injured shoulder but left without receiving treatment. They told police he seemed nervous and uneasy.

The hurt person used another person's identification and gave the clerk the fake name and a birthdate of May 12, 1946, which would have made him 31 years old at the time. He told her he worked for the Rice Growers and fell off scaffolding and hurt himself.

Investigators spoke to the person whose I.D. was used. The man's wallet was lost or stolen two years prior to the hospital incident. He presumed it was lost because none of the credit cards had been used. The man did work for the Rice Growers. This man was much older than the birthdate that the hurt person gave as 1946... most likely because the hurt person could not pull off the older age on the I.D.

After Attack #22, the EAR took a 13-week break from committing his usual attacks. This break from crime led Law Enforcement to believe the EAR was hurt and needed to heal before he returned to committing his crimes.

On the hospital paperwork were the initials, B.K., thought to be written by a hospital clerk. In 2016, Law Enforcement shared this information with the public in an attempt to gather more information to identify the clerk. Law Enforcement has since received information from a researcher who they believe was the clerk. She passed away before they were able to speak with her.

Yogi's real initials are B.K. Is this a coincidence or did Yogi put his initials down on the paperwork in the wrong place? Did the clerk and Yogi have the same initials?

I wonder if Joseph DeAngelo missed any work during this time. If it was DeAngelo who hurt himself trying to escape after the south Sacramento attack, why would he travel all the way to Carmichael for medical help two days later? He lived and worked as a police officer in Auburn at the time. He could have easily gone to a hospital in Auburn and told them he fell off his bike or some other believable lie. His own insurance would have covered the cost. It would have been too risky for a police officer to use a stolen ID and lie to the hospital staff. It makes no sense.

IT SCARES MOMMY

MY DAD LOVED A PRINCESS. HE LAUGHED AT HER JOKES, praised every piece of artwork she made, and protected her from all the witches in the world. I was that princess, and he was my everything. He was irreplaceable.

Nine years passed without my dad. At the private school, Mr. Clarke worked at trying to be my dad, but he turned out to be an imposter, unloving, and cruel.

Then Yogi came along. He was nothing like my father, but offered love, protection, and laughter. He appeared intelligent but he was really only street smart. At the time, I didn't know the difference.

I was an orphan and Yogi perceived he was one also. We used each other to fill in what was missing in our lives. He looked out for me like a father would do. Yogi and I played "Mommy and Son" when we goofed around. He talked and acted like a little boy, and I was his mommy. His birthday cards were always written as if he were my child. At the time, we didn't have any children. The game was silly, but upon reflection, I think it comforted him to have a "nice mommy," instead of one who gave him away and the other who abused him.

After rummaging, raping, and eating at the 22nd attack, the East Area Rapist cried for the first time. "It scares Mommy when it's on the news." he repeated to himself, and seemed to cry harder when he said, "Mommy."

This was one bit of information I wondered about. Was he talking about his adopted mother? No, he despised her, and he didn't say, "It scares my Ma." Did his natural mother fit this scenario? No, he didn't know his natural mother yet and wouldn't meet her for another three years. How would the attacks scare *either* mother when they were not aware of them? Yogi and I didn't have children at the time, so I wasn't a mother.

I wrestled with my next thought. Could I be the mommy he cried about? His pretend mommy? This idea disturbs me. As I piece together the puzzle, our sex life and partnership life were in many ways, Yogi's fantasy. I am afraid I already know the answer to that question.

Recently, I pulled my old boxes of photos and albums down from the top shelves in my bedroom closet. I rarely look at them because I'm usually too busy, and the boxes of photos remind me that I need to organize them. Out of sight, out of mind.

I pulled down the large brown photo album. This particular album only holds my family photos. I glanced at all of them, then turned to a page that held a handmade birthday card Yogi gave me over forty years ago. It surprised me to find it there, as this album is reserved for my family photos. The birthday card had been in that photo album all those years. I guess I never paid attention. The card has brown spots where possibly the acidic adhesive started to deteriorate the paper. All of this pushed memories to the floodgates, and they all crashed in like unstoppable waves. Just another corner piece to place in the Yogi puzzle.

THE FORGOTTEN VICTIM

THE COUPLE QUARRELED THAT SATURDAY NIGHT IN OCTOBER OF 1977, so he drove her home early. She was only seventeen, and he was not much older. They patched things up and headed back to the duplex on La Riviera Drive to spend the night at his place.

Not long after 1:00 a.m., the sleeping couple got an unexpected visitor. They both slept until the man with a nylon stocking over his face stood in their bedroom doorway. There's no telling how long he stood there holding his gun in his right hand and a flashlight in his left. Overcome with fear, the young girl woke her boyfriend. The intruder commanded them, "Shut up! Don't make a move or I'll kill you! I want your dope. I know you have some and I'll look until I find it."

When adrenaline is surging through your veins and fear is paralyzing your body, it's hard to make a quick decision on how to keep yourself alive. A shotgun leaned on the bedroom wall near the bed. The attacker played a little game with his victims. He shined his flashlight on the boyfriend, then on the shotgun. Back and forth. Back and forth. He goaded him into a duel. Turns out, the boyfriend was wise. He lay there still, taking the chance he and his girlfriend would make it through this ordeal alive.

The rapist ordered them on their stomachs. He tied them up, stacked dishes on the male's back and rummaged through the home looking for what he came for. When he returned to their bedroom, he walked the girl to the living room and raped her twice. He held his knife to her throat and threatened her. Several times the EAR held his gun to both of their heads and cocked it to increase their level of fear.

After the first time the EAR raped the young woman, the doorbell rang. The couple listened as the rapist opened the door and went outside. He returned inside to the woman, raped her again, then made his way to the kitchen. The couple heard a car horn honk a couple times, then honk again. Their doorbell rang five times and then someone knocked on their window. The female victim heard the whispers of the attacker and a woman whispering back through the window. Soon after, the attacker disappeared from the duplex.

There were other attacks when the East Area Rapist spoke or pretended to be speaking to another person. This particular time is different, with honking horns and door knocking.

They described the attacker as about 5 foot 9 inches tall and weighing about 170 pounds. He had bad breath and terrible body odor. He used a nylon stocking over his face with a dark cap on his head.

The seventeen-year-old girl worked at the Sixpence Hotel at the time of the attack. Is it possible Yogi spotted her when picking up or dropping off a fare in his cab to that hotel? She had a medical procedure done at a hospital in North Sacramento a few days before the attack. Was he working as a security guard then at the hospital? He could have seen her then, or he could have seen her weeks before the attack.

Detectives investigated the crime scene and discovered something eerie. Someone removed the boyfriend's shotgun shells from his gun and lined them up under his bed. The duplex was empty earlier when the couple drove to her apartment. Was the EAR in the house earlier staging his rape fantasy? Did he make sure he would remain safe during his visit by removing those shells? No wonder he invited the male to a duel.

The EAR had never attacked anyone in a duplex before. It had all the bells and whistles that he liked. A levee road behind the duplex, an apartment complex, a school, and a pedestrian overpass were all nearby, making it easy to move away from the area.

There's that body odor and bad breath again. Yogi's calling card from time to time. Yogi was far from being considered an unkempt person. He showered twice a day and seemed obsessive about his clothing. After laundering, his clothing was carefully folded and placed neatly in his dresser drawers. He is the only person I've known to iron creases in his jeans. But he had little control over his body odor after exerting even a small amount of energy.

Forty-three years later, the boyfriend spoke during the victim impact statements before Joseph DeAngelo's sentencing. The gentleman felt like a forgotten male victim. He was angry. He expressed to all how disappointed he was with law enforcement. The night of the rape, one male and two female officers showed up to take a report. The two officers laughed in the kitchen, while two young victims tried to make sense of what happened to them. It was just minutes after the two had wondered whether they would make it past that night after being violated by the East Area Rapist.

The boyfriend handed the judge a copy of an Auburn City Police Log. He said it showed Joseph DeAngelo worked at the Auburn Police Department the night he broke into his home on October 1, 1977. His opinion was that Law Enforcement knew abo DeAngelo committing crimes during the time he worked for the police department.

In my opinion, if Joseph DeAngelo worked that night at the Auburn Police Department, it would have been unlikely for him to commit this crime. The estimated time committing the crime was one hour and forty-five minutes inside the residence. The commute time from the Auburn area to Rancho Cordova in the 1970s, traffic considered, was about an hour and twenty minutes, round trip. The East Area Rapist spent a significant amount of time surveying his victims and their homes. Add in the time to enter the home, unload the shotgun, and place the shells under the bed. Considering this timeline, DeAngelo would have had to spend a considerable amount of his shift committing this crime. Could he take this many hours out of his shift without his employer or fellow employees knowing? Could he be away from his radio for that length of time? Would DeAngelo bust in and demand dope?

In the 1970s, it would be no problem to drive a cab during the night shift and do whatever you pleased. The only link between you and your employer was a radio in your vehicle. If you didn't answer, the dispatcher gave other drivers the fare and would ignore you the rest of the night.

Most security guards carried pagers. It was rare for the security company to page a guard while he was on duty. I am not sure whether Yogi worked as a security guard or a cab driver at the time of this attack, but I do know it was one or the other.

On October 1, 2018, Steve Large, a reporter with Channel 13 News, interviewed the male survivor in this attack. He told the reporter he remembered the pants worn by the rapist the night he attacked them. "I know what police-issued khaki trousers look like. And the ones worn by the attacker were light tan in color, or a shade of green." Steve Large reported that the Auburn Police Department wore light blue uniforms in the 70s.

As the reporter and the young girl's boyfriend walked along the levee behind the duplex, I was reminded of the walks that Yogi and I took in Massachusetts. The boyfriend told the reporter that the cops would show up on La Riviera Drive and he was already on the other side of the river. Déjà vu.

It might not have been Joseph DeAngelo inside the duplex that night back in October 1977. Perhaps it wasn't a police officer. It's possible a security guard or cab driver paid the young couple a visit that autumn evening.

LITTLE BLUE FLAKES

THE BLUE APARTMENTS GOT A FRESH LOOK BEFORE
WE MOVED TO P STREET. The pitiful place had seen better days.
The exterior of the building was cracking and peeling and begged for
a new coat of paint while I begged for a new color.

The paint crew worked in every corner of the building, mostly sanding. After a while, the sanding became a real nuisance. Tiny blue specks
were sprinkled all over the porch, sidewalks, and the covered garage
under the building on O Street. Those little blue specks hitchhiked on
every foot that entered the building and into every apartment, I'm sure.
Our cats were even guilty of bringing them inside.

Investigators found traces of blue paint at three of the East Area
Rapist attacks. Blue paint flakes showed up in the victim's bedding at
Attack #25. At Attack #26 investigators found blue flakes in the living
room, bedroom, and closet. Traces were found in the victim's hair and
on shoelaces. Blue flakes appeared on a pair of boots, shoelaces, and in
the vacuum bag at Attack #27.

Law enforcement described the blue flakes as "microscopic chips of
blue architectural paint that likely came from a paint sprayer." It was a
flat paint, not glossy and contained silicates, phthalo, and lead. Silicates
in the paint would help repel dirt and water would roll off the building

when it rained. It's referred to as the "lotus effect." Painting contractors used this type of paint on exterior buildings only. Investigators reasoned that the East Area Rapist was either a painter or worked in construction. Unfortunately, law enforcement disposed of all the physical evidence pertaining to the East Area Rapist cases many years ago.

I was reminded of The Blue Apartments and the invasion of blue flakes of paint caused by all the sanding that took place. When my cursor hit the page with the sample color of paint flakes online, my jaw dropped. The paint color matched The Blue Apartments trim color perfectly. I have to wonder if the blue flakes of paint found at three attacks belong to The Blue Apartments.

Today a beige blanket with white trim drapes the old Blue Apartments, but I know there is a strange blue color underneath it all, over forty years deep.

THE MAGGIORE MURDERS

SHOTS RANG OUT OVER LA ALEGRIA DRIVE IN RANCHO
CORDOVA after 9:00 p.m. Neighbors peered out their windows, and
some raced outside to find out what happened. Bullets struck Brian and
Katie Maggiore down in their own quiet neighborhood. They were a
young newlywed couple. Brian, 21, was an Air Force Sergeant stationed
at the Mather Field Air Force Base. Katie, 20, grew up in Fresno,
California and worked at a gas station nearby.

On February 2, 1978, Mr. and Mrs. Maggiore took their little gray
poodle, Thumper, for a walk. They weren't far from their apartment
that Thursday evening. I picture the two exchanging the events of their
day as they walked along their neighborhood streets. A jogger passed by
them along the way. The jogger witnessed a man standing near some
bushes on West La Loma Drive. He described him as having curly
brown hair and wearing a brown padded jacket.

A few weeks before the double murder, neighbors dealt with crank
phone calls, peeping toms, and prowling activity. They found opened
gates and footprints in many yards. Burglaries were on the rise. A burglar broke into a woman's home and stole her underwear.

The Maggiore couple ended up in the backyard of a home on La
Alegria Drive. No one is sure why. Law enforcement suspects the two

might have witnessed the shooter lurking around homes. A ten-year-old boy peered out his second-story window and witnessed the shooter firing a shot at the couple. He stared as the shooter fired another shot toward the patio. They found Brian in this area on the ground. He suffered wounds to his chest and neck. Katie ran for her life, shouting, "Help me!" She reached a gate, but found it locked. The killer caught up to Katie and shot her in the head. They found Thumper, the poodle, in the swimming pool in the backyard. He was later retrieved, still alive, from the pool. The witness watched the shooter run around the side of the house and disappear.

A few homes down from the shooting, Karl Nollsch, a seventeen-year-old, heard the loud booms. He dashed outside to his driveway to investigate the noise. As he glanced to his left, he discovered someone come over the gate and watched as he sprinted toward him. When the shooter noticed Karl standing there, he rushed the opposite direction and around a corner. Karl stood about five feet from him. The killer wore a ski mask, dark pants, soft shoes, and carried a gun in his right hand. The ski mask exposed the eyes and nose of the perpetrator. He was a white male, 6 ft.- 6 ft. 2 inches, and between 28-30 years old. His brown jacket had a 5 inch long and 2-inch-wide stain on the lower right back side. The stain resembled the shape of a peanut.

The Sheriff's Department shared this statement with the public. They said, "Several other witnesses saw the same suspect (based upon their general agreement on clothing description and other features) on Capitales Drive and other nearby streets heading northeast, away from the crime scene. By this point, the suspect had removed his ski mask, and held it in his hands. Several of the witnesses noted odd behavior, including strange comments such as, 'Excuse me, I'm trespassing' when seen by a resident in their yard. One witness said the suspect looked like he carried a football-sized object in his hand that looked like cloth. The suspect would jump behind objects and shield his face with his arm and jacket whenever he encountered a witness. Another witness saw the grip of a handgun protruding from the right rear pocket of his pants."

Another neighbor was certain the EAR's description of 6 ft.-6 ft. 2 inches was incorrect. She stated she viewed it all from across the street. She matched her neighbor's height to the gunman's height and to a spot on the tree in the yard. The woman told police he stood only about 5 ft.9 inches.

Prior to the murders, Katie complained she was being stalked by someone while at work. She worked at the Regal Gas Station nearby. She also received phone calls from a male warning, "Your turn is coming."

They rushed Katie and Brian to the hospital where they both died. DNA wasn't available to collect. Police found a pre-tied dark blue shoelace twelve feet from Brian's body. It resembled the tied ligature the East Area Rapist used to tie his victims. Law enforcement released little information on this case. They didn't share information with other departments. Without up-to-date information, homicide detectives did not link these horrific murders to the East Area Rapist for another twenty years.

The only conclusion that we can draw from these murders is that Katie and Brian must have seen the shooter's face and could identify him. The shooter might have been in the middle of prowling or stalking someone. Police are of the opinion that the murder was not intentional.

The killer's agility and physical description matched the East Area Rapist. The neighborhood was his usual territory. Another clue was the blue shoelace found near Brian's body.

Brian and Katie's murders were senseless. Is it possible Yogi was the shooter? Although I find it hard to believe Yogi would be an intentional killer, I can picture him hurting someone to protect his identity. The Marine Corps trained him how to use weapons and to kill to protect.

Witnesses described the shooter as having curly brown hair. Yogi's hair was curly and brown. He had large curls when his hair was on the longer side. They described him as a White male in his mid-twenties, wearing dark pants and dark shoes. The killer held the weapon in his right hand and carried it in his right rear pocket. Yogi was right-handed. Joseph DeAngelo is left-handed.

There is no DNA evidence for these murders. The only evidence we know of is the blue shoelace that was found twelve feet from Brian Maggiore. Extensive prowling occurred in the weeks that led up to the murders. Twelve homes in the vicinity reported prowling. The murders were near previous rape Attacks #1, #3, #6, #8, and #15.

———

I listened intently as the Sacramento County Deputy DA described what led up to the murders of Brian and Katie Maggiore. He spoke at Joseph DeAngelo's hearing. He described what witnesses saw before the shooting. As the Maggiore's walked along La Alegria and West La Loma, a seventeen-year-old jogger sprinted past them. "The jogger saw a white male wearing a brown padded jacket hiding in the dark near some bushes in front of a house on the opposite side of the street." If the Maggiore couple continued the same path, they would have met up with this male. The Deputy DA did not mention that the suspicious White male had curly brown hair. Why? Joseph DeAngelo's hair was straight and blonde to light brown.

THE MINNOW HOLE

THOMAS ALWAYS TUCKED HIS MOOD AWAY FROM MOST PEOPLE, but somehow, he allowed me to know that private part of him. I felt like his sister. He was about to purchase his first home, and nothing he did could hide his pride.

Thomas' eyes danced as he told Yogi and me that he bought a house in the southern area of Sacramento. Although we couldn't relate, we were happy for him. This meant he would move from a duplex on 38th Street. His plan became more exciting because it made it possible for us to rent that duplex.

Thomas would have to wait for escrow to close on his home, so he moved into his parents' home where he stored his larger belongings. It allowed Yogi and me to move into the place on 38th Street. The duplex was the first unfurnished place we rented, so Thomas let us use his things until his new home closed escrow.

Thomas' home was about five miles from the Little Pocket area. It was about five miles from downtown Sacramento, and Interstate 5 bordered the east side. On the south, west, and north, the Sacramento River bends around in a semicircle. It looks like a pocket on the map, so the neighborhood is called Little Pocket. On April 14, 1978, it jolted this neighborhood to hear the news of Attack #31.

It was close to 9:00 p.m. when a fifteen-year-old girl arrived at Casilada Way, Sacramento, to babysit. She put the young child to bed and started watching a movie. The garage door was busted open by a masked man. With his teeth clenched, the criminal told her not to move or he would kill her. He held a gun to her head.

The EAR kept with his normal M.O. When the telephone rang, it threw him off his plan. He left the room until the phone became silent again. Again, the phone rang. The rapist picked up the phone and forced the young girl to answer the call. When she said, "Hello," he hung up on the caller.

The telephone rang a third time because the caller wasn't giving up. This time the rapist pushed the girl outside into the backyard. Her father drove up and called out the young girl's name. In no time, the EAR was long gone. They contacted police and soon the tracking dogs showed up, along with a helicopter.

Distraught, the girl didn't give police many details of the rapist. He wore a blue plaid shirt, gloves, and a mask, and held an ice pick in his right hand. The rapist left at 10:00 p.m.

Fifteen minutes after the attack, at 10:15 p.m. a witness saw a man jogging on the levee at Minnow Hole. He was about 25 years old, of medium build and about 5 foot 8 inches tall. The man had brown collar-length hair and a brown mustache.

Minnow Hole is a popular fishing spot south of Little Pocket in Sacramento. He passed by a woman fishing. Out of breath, he asked her if she caught any fish yet. "No, I didn't get any."

"Oh, my wife is going to be mad," he said as he jogged off in a hurry. The woman thought it was strange that the man wasn't wearing jogging clothes, and he was out of breath as if he had been running. It seemed a ploy to make it seem as if he needed to get home fast.

Yogi was partial to walking along levees after committing crimes. There were only two ways out of the Little Pocket area. North of the pocket and south of the pocket. Parking a car inside the pocket would prove dangerous during a getaway for an attacker. It would be too easy for police to block you in. But if you parked outside of the Little Pocket area and walked along the levee to your car, your escape would be easier. This is what he did.

The man who passed the woman at Minnow Hole was moving south. This direction is a logical direction if Yogi's goal was the Meadowview Terrace neighborhood where Thomas' home was pending. Thomas' escrow closed in June 1978.

This attack happened earlier in the evening than most of the other attacks. Yogi matched the jogger's description from his brown hair and mustache right down to the flannel blue, plaid shirt. The time causes me to wonder if Yogi stopped by Thomas' new home that evening to take a look at the home. The EAR favored using vacant homes for temporary lairs near many of his attacks. Was Thomas' home vacant during escrow?

The East Area Rapist attacked in this area only once. After this failed attack, he laid low for a couple months and returned to attacking out of the Sacramento area. Law Enforcement was no closer to catching the rapist than they were thirty attacks ago. So, they plodded along in hopes of changing that disappointing fact.

CALLOUSED THUMBS

TO QUELL HIS DESIRES IN TERRORIZING TEENAGED GIRLS, THE EAST AREA RAPIST moved on to Modesto for his 32nd attack. The young couple woke to the masked perpetrator shining his flashlight in their eyes. He brought his own shoelaces and ordered them on their stomachs. The young woman tied her husband and like always, the EAR re-tied him tighter. He tied the female and brought her to another room. He placed dishes on the husband and told the couple he only wanted money and food. The stranger returned to the husband to taunt him by telling him he was going to rape his wife. He sexually assaulted the young woman.

The couple told police the rapist smelled like beer and used a fake Spanish accent. They overheard him pacing the floor and crying. He was White, in his twenties, and fit. They said judging by what he said and how he said it, the rapist appeared undereducated.

By the couple's description, it sounds like Yogi paid them a visit that night.

The East Area Rapist spent the summer of 1978 attacking in the Davis and Modesto area. Prior to Attack #33, the apartment janitor witnessed a stranger staring at one of the female residents at the pool. A few days later the same young girl viewed a White male with a mustache watching her at the mailboxes. The descriptions of this man were the same. He stood about six feet tall and wore his dark brown hair brushed back. The description resembled the man seen in the Little Pocket Area after Attack #31.

At almost four o'clock in the morning on June 7th, 1978, the EAR assaulted a twenty-one-year-old college student in her apartment. She fought back and he brutally beat her. He pulled her hair, broke her nose, punched her, and stabbed her with a nail file. His description matched the lurking stranger at the pool and mailboxes.

The woman watched the rapist removed his gloves. She felt his calloused thumbs and short nails on her body. Yogi chewed his nails down to the quick. So badly, his fingers bled. The resin from smoking weed stained Yogi's thumbs yellow. Relighting his pipe with a lighter caused calluses on his thumbs.

On a Friday evening in June 1978, a cab driver sat waiting for his next fare at an airport in Modesto. His next fare arrived and wanted to go to "Sylvan and Coffee." The cab driver described the person as a White male, about thirty years old, with light brown hair carrying one piece of luggage. He had a medium build and stood about 5 foot 9 inches. The cab driver dropped him off about half a mile from Attack #34. The man got out of the cab and walked through a field carrying his bag. There were homes under construction in the area.

The East Area Rapist used his repertoire of actions with this couple as he did with the others before. Before retiring to bed, the couple made sure they locked every window and door in their home. They believe the rapist made his way in through the kitchen sliding door because there were no signs of forced entry. During the attack, they heard his zippered bag opening and closing. He stole their wedding rings and a .357 Magnum. The couple described him to be under six feet tall, slender build, and in his early twenties. He spoke with a fake Spanish accent.

The young couple had only been living in their new home for a couple of months. The neighborhood was still under construction with some other homes around them. During construction of homes or apartments, the general contractor uses one key that allows access to all the homes. They call it a "construction key" or "master key." After the homes receive a certificate of occupancy, they rekey the locks. Is it possible the contractor missed this home? Or a group of homes? The perpetrator most likely used a key. Security guards usually had access to the construction keys when workers were away from the construction site.

There were several attacks on or near construction sites. Too many thefts occurred when the sites were empty. If the perpetrator was the guy who took the cab, he knew what he was doing. The pick-up point was the airport, and the drop off was a street corner. It looks like the rapist didn't want anyone in that neighborhood to see his car, especially if that car brought the security guard to his job every night and parked there most nights. And especially if that car was a loud Ford Torino with a crazy paint job.

The rapist woke the victims of the 35th attack with his flashlight and a .357 Magnum in their two-story home. He barked his normal orders and told them, "All I want is food and money. Food and money. I got to have money for gas. I got to have food." After the young woman tied her husband, the EAR tied the woman. He left the room to search for money.

The couple's young son got up to go to the bathroom, but he met the stranger in the hallway. He pushed the child into the bathroom and placed a cup and saucer on the doorknob. The stranger proceeded with his predictable M.O. When he forced the woman to masturbate him, he touched her back softly. When he forced her to orally copulate him, his hand moved the hair from her face. He raped her and afterwards, he cried.

The attack happened close to the UC Davis private airfield. The tracking dogs led police to an area where the EAR most likely parked his car, about two miles from the home.

The couple told investigators he had a medium build, big thighs, and his butt was hairy.

On October 13, 1978, the masked man woke the sleeping couple by barging through their bedroom door and blinding them with the light of his flashlight. They became the victims of his 36th attack. He told them, "I just want food and money for my girlfriend and me." When the woman's daughter woke and entered the couple's bedroom, the intruder forced her to the bathroom where he barricaded her in with furniture. He threatened the male victim with a gun and said, "All we want is food and money and then we'll get the hell out of here." He forced the woman to masturbate him, then raped her.

The intruder walked back and forth into the garage with a large bag. The victim overheard him tell someone, "Here, put this in the car." Investigators aren't sure whether there was a second person at the crime or if it was a hoax. A few homes down from the victims, a neighbor heard beeps coming from a car at the same time the rape occurred.

Throughout the East Area Rapist's reign of terror, there are several instances where investigators wondered about two perpetrators committing the crime together. Or were these just red herrings?

THE LOST BADGE

"DAMN, DAMN, DAMN-IT. WHERE IS THE DAMN THING?"

"Check the laundry, Yogi." In a frenzy, he searched for his security badge.

"I looked everywhere. It's fucking gone!" He kept picking up the same things and throwing them down. His blue eyes darted around the entire apartment. You could tell he was thinking hard. Really hard. Any minute, I expected billows of smoke to come rolling out of his ears and the aroma of burnt oil would fill the room. His nervous habit of clicking his teeth showed up instead. That got me up out of my chair to help him look.

Our searching was fruitless. Yogi told me the security company would charge him twenty dollars for a replacement badge. Twenty dollars bought a lot of bologna back then.

The company Yogi worked for was the largest security company in Sacramento and the surrounding area. He had an unblemished record, except for his juvenile record, so he had no problem getting hired.

The guards at this company wore brown uniforms, and darker brown pants with a lighter brown shirt. Yogi usually wore his black square-toed shoes when he worked for security companies.

The badge looked like a police officer's badge and felt heavier than the other badges Yogi had worn for smaller companies. He marveled at it and mentioned how realistic it looked. The company didn't hand out new clothing, jackets, and badges for employees to keep. They loaned these items out, but when the employee left the company, they had to return the items in order to receive their last paycheck.

The company loaned out a brown winter jacket that gathered at the waist. The material appeared shiny. There weren't any emblems sewn on the jacket that would announce he worked for a security company. Yogi only wore the badge on his shirt.

The East Area Rapist broke into the home of a couple on October 7,1978, making them victims of the 37th attack. He turned on the television, then covered it with a blanket, to create a low lighting effect. He ransacked the home several times, as usual, then raped the young woman. Afterward, he cowered in a corner of the living room and cried. The couple told police that he smelled like cinnamon.

The East Area Rapist hauled out thousands of dollars of houseware items during this attack, more than usual. He stole utensils, small appliances, dishware, and salt and pepper shakers, and other household items. Investigators thought the perpetrator stole the items to set up a new residence. The other possibility was fencing items to make money.

The attack occurred in Concord, California, about an hour away from Sacramento. From Sacramento, the EAR would have driven through Davis, Vacaville, and Fairfield before reaching Concord. In the past he attacked in Davis, but he didn't attack in Vacaville and Fairfield; at least not that we know about.

A neighbor found a security guard badge in her yard after the attack. Police searched the neighborhood for the owner just in case someone living nearby lost it. It didn't belong to anyone who lived on the block. The badge looked realistic. It was a mass-produced security badge manufactured on the east coast and sold to several security guard companies across the United States. It had been well used because it showed wear with many scratches. Law enforcement checked many security companies in Contra Costa and surrounding areas to see if they recognized the badge. They never found the company that used it. I wonder if they checked the Sacramento area. Can you imagine a security company owning up to the use of the badge? It might have confirmed they hired the EAR. That might not have been good for business.

Well, I don't think I have to tell you whose security badge I presume they found. Yogi's employer replaced his badge with another one. I wished I had asked him how he lost it. I always took the badge off the shirt to launder it each shift, as his body odor always reeked of sweat. Yogi put the badge back on the shirt before leaving for work. He must have removed the badge from his shirt before he arrived home. For what reason? Did he want to hide the fact he was a security guard?

Thomas was thoughtful to leave most of his belongings for us to use after he moved from the duplex. His home closed escrow toward the end of June 1978. Of course, he wanted his own kitchen items and other things returned to furnish his new home.

Yogi and I didn't have the money to purchase everything a person needs to set up a household. Periodically, he went to thrift stores to get the things we needed. Was Yogi filling our place with stolen items? That thought did not cross my mind at the time. Who would do such a thing? Yet, the time of this last attack was so close to the time Thomas moved into his new home and needed his kitchen items returned.

Many wondered why the rapist smelled like cinnamon. In the 70s, they made dime-store cologne for men. Because of Yogi's sweating problem, he used colognes often. The smell didn't last very long but it helped mask the odor of sweat. A set of Skin Bracer colognes sold back then had a pleasant smell. Yogi kept his bottles lined up on the back of the toilet. His cheap colognes were Skin Bracer, Cool Spice, and Winter Spice.

Many questioned why the East Area Rapist who attacked in the Sacramento area skipped over a few large cities and ended up in the city of Concord. My guess is that Yogi drove directly to Concord because he had a job as a security guard there. There were no attacks in the cities of Vacaville or Fairfield, cities one would pass through to get to Concord. They would have been closer cities if the EAR had just been interested in just getting out of the Sacramento area. Yogi did a lot of out-of-town security work in the seventies.

IT'S CRYING TIME AGAIN

THE THING ABOUT LOSERS IS THAT NOT ONLY DO THEY LOSE AT everything, but they also cause you to do the same. It's a mindset they love to share with their partners. And if you're not careful, you're thinking just like them. I tried to stay positive throughout my life. Even if I had to fake it, I did it until I believed it myself. I hoped I had enough positivity for both Yogi and me.

We got our second television, but I wondered how long that would last. We lost the first one to the pawnshop. I can't explain where our money went. I never asked because most of the time I wasn't the one working. I stayed busy with school and homework and never missed it. Still, it's hard to see you're making progress in life when you can't even keep your television on the shelf.

The East Area Rapist was regular in his attacks. However, looking at his timelines, there were 3-month intervals between some of his attacks. Some believe he might have used the time for stalking other areas and victims. Some said it looked like a school schedule. The intervals were summer and winter break.

The EAR never needed three months to prepare to attack. He might have laid low when the heat was on, but looking at the timeline, that doesn't seem to fit that scenario. I have another theory.

Yogi didn't attend college, but I did. I attended Sacramento City College. I went to school during the day, studied at night, and went to bed early when school was in session. During winter and summer breaks, I stayed up later and was home during the day. My time off would have put a damper on his stalking. It's possible Yogi's attack timeline coincided with my school schedule:

5/17/1977 Attack #21
5/28/1977 Attack #22
No attacks for 3 months
9/6/1977 Attack #23
6/24/1978 Attack #35
7/6/1978 Attack #36
No attacks for 3 months
10/7/1978 Attack #37
12/2/1978 Attack #41
12/9/1978 Attack #42
No attacks for 3 months
3/20/1979

I slept better on P Street. Our bedroom was up a flight of stairs and down a long hallway. It was far enough from the living room so when Yogi went into one of his fits of scratching his head feverishly, crying, and squealing at his ma, I didn't hear it unless I was awake.

Several nights I laid in bed listening to the commotion going on in Yogi's head. It's a pathetic sound because you realize that is exactly where it originated. It's all in his head, and he couldn't escape. I felt helpless knowing he had to face his demons by himself. I didn't know how to help him. And he didn't want my help. It was his thing, and he would handle it. Although the earlier I went to bed, the easier it was to ignore it.

"BECAUSE I'M HUNGRY"

THE EAST AREA RAPIST HELD HIS KNIFE UP TO THE TEMPLE OF THE WOMAN and ordered her not to make a sound or he would kill her. She became #40. The 34-year-old woman screamed and cried.

"Don't you understand?" he questioned her. He told her all he wanted was food and money. He tied her hands and feet and ripped up towels to use as a gag and blindfolds, then raped her. The rapist spent an hour in her home.

About the only information police gleaned from this attack was that the rapist carried a knife and had a small penis. She also told them she thought he was Asian but couldn't expand on why. The victim was Asian. If the rapist was Yogi, could it be that he led her to believe he was Asian? A whispered word? Did he use a Japanese pitch accent when he spoke? The police did not consider the attack an 'East Area Rapist Attack' until later. According to everything I have read about this case, it is evident to me that the police didn't investigate this attack well.

Almost a month went by, and the EAR attacked his 41st victim in San Jose. He worked hard to enter this home. They found wood chippings on the garage man-door, broken glass from a bedroom window, and broken glass from a living room window. He ended up going through the sliding glass door.

In the middle of the night of December 2, 1978, the East Area Rapist abruptly woke up his victims. The woman screamed, and the husband bolted from the bed. The masked man hit him in the shins with his gun and yelled, "Don't move, Motherfucker. You try that again, Motherfucker, and I'll shoot you."

The intruder made sure the woman could breathe easily with the gag in her mouth. There were other instances the EAR showed kindness, if that is what you can call it, during some of his horrendous rapes.

"I only want money and food because I'm hungry," he said, then continued with his normal M.O. When he finished raping the woman he cried, "You Motherfucker. You Motherfucker." He left the woman and checked in on her husband in the other room. He returned to the woman and raped her again. The rapist returned to the kitchen and cried out loud, "This attack is the last time!"

The wife told police that the rapist's penis was five or six inches long. Both thought he was Black because of the way he said, "Motherfucker." He seemed to be in his twenties. He stole money, a ring, and a six-pack of Coors. She worked as a registered nurse at nearby Stanford Hospital.

———

The East Area Rapist was back in Rancho Cordova for Attack #43. She was a single mom. It was March 20, 1979. When she screamed out, he brutally hit her with an object several times. The mother told police he was about 6 foot and weighed about one-hundred-eighty pounds. This perpetrator was heavier than the previous rapists. She said he tried to speak with a deeper voice and spoke slowly, maybe to cover a stutter.

The masked stranger used a cord from her garage to tie her and put a scarf in her mouth instead of the usual ripped towel. He didn't use shoelaces in this attack. When he noticed a large scar on her back, he ended the attack and didn't rape her.

The attack wasn't in the usual part of Rancho Cordova where he invaded his victims. It was located almost three miles away.

From Rancho Cordova to Fremont, California is where the rapist landed For Attack #44. He entered through the sliding glass door after trying several ways to get in the house.

"Motherfucker, you're dead. Put your face down or I'll blow your fucking head off." He used many items to restrain the boyfriend: a necktie, shoelaces, nylons, and an electrical cord. The boyfriend was larger than the stranger.

The female told authorities his penis was only about three inches. He was in his late twenties to early thirties, about 5 ft. 8 inches to 6 ft. The twenty-seven-year-old woman informed police that his hands were soft and not calloused.

50 PSYCHICS 1978

YOGI AND I SANG AS WE SQUARE DANCED TO THE
THEME SONG OF 'THE JEFFERSONS' TV SHOW. When
Yogi parked the car in our new driveway, we felt we "had arrived."
It was a stone's throw from downtown Sacramento. Lush, mature
trees with manicured lawns lined 38th Street. Our new address was in
east Sacramento. Our new place sat a few homes from the end of the
dead-end street. Traffic turned out to be almost nonexistent. After
we parked, I took my shoes off and ran to the lawn. The grass felt
glorious on my bare feet. Many years had passed since my feet felt the
soft blades of grass between my toes. I had been living in the city way
too long.

    Yogi popped the trunk open, and we lifted our bags of clothes and
toiletries out of the Torino. That's all we had. The only downfall of
renting a furnished apartment is when your next place is unfurnished.
For this move, we needed to buy pots, pans, dishes, and bedroom, dining and living room furniture. The list of things seemed endless. But
it was worth it. Thomas left us some of his furniture, like the bed and
some dishes to use, until we could get our own. We used a large and
sturdy cardboard box for our television stand. The small twelve-inch
TV sat centered on the box as if it was on top of a Regency brass inlaid

side table. Across from the television sat a ragged, worn-out green velour sofa for those comfy nights of television watching for two.

We settled in quickly and our outlook turned hopeful. The old wooden floors and built-in china cabinets gave the place a character of its own. When I moved into a new place, I always wondered what went on there before we claimed it as our home. Did love and laughter fill this room or did an older person gaze out the same window I'm looking through? I pictured years of happy memories in this very house, and I believed Yogi and I were about to make some new ones.

The dilapidated wooden garage was on our side of the duplex at the end of our driveway. Behind the garage it looked like someone once had a vegetable garden, but an assortment of tall weeds laid claim to the area. Beyond the back of the property, a dirt road served as an alleyway for 38th and 39th Street. One of our bedroom windows faced the driveway near the garage, and another window faced the backyard toward the alleyway.

In the middle of the night, I woke to a strange sound coming from the backyard. Did someone just open our garage door? It sounded like wood dragging on the cement, but only a light scrape. My cat's head turned toward the garage door and her ears perked up. She knew something crept out there in the dark, and I knew it too. We both sat listening intently for another sound, which never came while we remained awake. After a few minutes, she laid down and fell asleep. Then I did the same.

The next morning, I checked the garage door and backyard for anything out of place. On the trampled path from the alleyway to our backyard, I found black flex ties lying on the ground. I wasn't sure what they were at first, but after looking them over, I figured out their use. I was nervous knowing some uninvited creep poked around my backyard that evening. Yogi didn't seem phased about them at all. After taking a brief look at it, he tossed the ties in the garbage. Now I wonder if Yogi came through our backyard from the alleyway and dropped them that night.

During Attack #45, the East Area Rapist used flex ties to bind the seventeen-year-old girl in Walnut Creek. It was the summer of 1979. This was the only time he used these types of ties. The rapist lay on top of her and asked, "Have you ever fucked before?" He couldn't penetrate her vagina. He forced her to masturbate him with her hands tied behind her back. The masked stranger bit one of her nipples hard, then raped her.

The young teen described the rapist as 5 ft. 6 inches, and no fat on his body. His dark windbreaker had white lettering on the left side front of his jacket.

Could the flex ties be the same ties I found in my backyard in the summer of 1979?

———

Betty's mother helped her find a new job as a residential manager of a small property in Carmichael. The job seemed perfect for her. Managing the twenty-two-unit apartments turned out to be the break she needed.

By this time Betty and Yogi tolerated each other well. They both got used to the little idiosyncrasies of each other's personality. One time she gave Yogi a blue lightweight windbreaker that someone from her carpet cleaning company left at the apartments. On the left pocket side of the jacket was Custom Carpet Care in white lettering. Could this be the same dark windbreaker with white lettering the young teen saw during Attack #45?

On a beautiful day in June of 1979, I found out our lives were about to change in a big way. I missed my period, which either meant I was pregnant, or my body was just teasing me. Sure enough, the doctor told me my bundle of joy would arrive in January 1980. We both felt the excitement of bringing a son or daughter into our lives. But with that, also came a certain reluctance. Are we ready? Are we prepared? Can we afford it? And how do you even take care of a baby? The only baby I knew was my next-door neighbor's baby. I watched and learned everything I could from her. She made it look manageable. It's a good thing too, because they moved to a different city before our son was born.

Our neighbors bought a mobile home and started moving their things. I was just leaving their side of the duplex when the husband walked to the front door. "Hey, do you or Yogi have anything in the garage?"

"No way," I said.

"I found a box that's not ours," he told me.

"What's in it?" I asked.

"Ski masks, some dishes, and a bunch of other items."

"Nope, not ours."

He shrugged his shoulders and said, "Ahh, must belong to the owner then."

I never gave it another thought; that is, until years later.

I stayed connected with Carla and let her know the other half of the duplex was going to be vacant. She got a job transfer, packed her car, and left Oceanside. In no time, she was our next-door neighbor. I enjoyed having her around again, but she worked so much I didn't get to see her as often as I would have liked.

Law enforcement hired over 50 psychics to use their supernatural powers to find the East Area Rapist. Fifty. They were at their wit's end. They just couldn't get a grip on the EAR. He seemed unstoppable. I know nothing about psychics, but these visions are, if nothing else, interesting.

In Detective Richard Shelby's book, "Hunting A Psychopath," he talks about a hired psychic that saw the rapist go to an old home and kept all his rape things in an old shed behind the house. The home had wooden steps to the door. She said there was an old woman in the house that he hated. The psychic was not far off. If her vision was of Yogi's home in Massachusetts with his gray-haired mother whom he hated, she was on point. Behind the house he grew up was an old, dilapidated garage. Maybe when he was younger, Yogi hid his burglary tools and spoils there.

If the psychic saw the duplex on 38th Street in her vision, she was close. They built the duplex in 1925 on 18 acres. The detached garage was original to the home. The rickety old wooden door scraped the cement, making a horrible noise unless you lifted it to close. Cobwebs, mildew smells, and boxes of junk were the only things in it. We shared the garage with our neighbors on the other side of the duplex. To my knowledge, we stored nothing in that garage. It was a perfect hiding place. I certainly wouldn't look there for anything. I entered one time when we first moved in and decided I wouldn't do that again.

———

Yogi's biological mother, Shirley, had him out of wedlock in the early 1950s. She struggled with public sentiment, her religion, work, and her family. Her family introduced her to a wonderful Catholic family with two older children. The couple wanted another baby to love.

Shirley kept in touch with Yogi's new parents throughout the years to hear about his milestones in life. They introduced Shirley as Aunt Shirley and Yogi was a huge fan of this loving and gregarious woman.

It wouldn't be until just before our son, Benjamin, was born that Yogi would find out the truth about who his mother was. Shirley seemed far too interested throughout my pregnancy and how Yogi and I were doing. One day I asked her directly. "Shirley, are you Yogi's mother?" My impatience grew with her silence. I heard a giggle and she proudly said, "Yes! Yes, I am!" The three of us couldn't contain our happiness.

I fell in love with Shirley two minutes after talking with her. Yogi inherited her funny genes. We both loved her and felt we couldn't have picked a better person to be Benjamin's grandma.

Shirley was a mover and a shaker. She filled a quiet room with laughter the minute she stepped in. She stayed involved with her church and community. She sang beautifully and loved being involved in theatre. Shirley retired as a nurse due to health issues. She never married or had any other children.

It was a magnificent early morning when the 8-pound 9-ounce little man arrived in our lives. My old neighbor friend met us at the hospital and helped me through the hard parts. It only took four hours and there he was. The entire world stopped in time when I gazed at the small, sweet person in my arms, and I realized he was a part of me. He was perfect. I instantly fell madly in love with him.

In junior high school I had a crush on the cutest boy in the world. His name was Benjamin. There was a sparkle in every girl's eye that glanced his way. He strutted through the halls of my school like a teen idol. I looked at him with dreamy eyes and promised myself, "When I grow up and have a little baby boy, I am going to name him Benjamin." And I did. It was my secret, of course, until now.

I never would have dreamed Benjamin would only be in this world for twenty years. He grew up a kind, funny, and a loving person. He always protected the underdog – in any situation.

When Benjamin was twenty, he hung out with the wrong crowd. He experimented with smoking 'crank' and became addicted. It was his demise. Benjamin passed away from an overdose. To top it off, the worst thing a mother could experience in her lifetime is to learn that her son smoked crank with his father. That was Benjamin. Instead of being part of the solution, Yogi was part of the problem. I've searched but I'm unable to find the right words or enough words to describe the loss of my son. Twenty-one years after Benjamin's death, the memory is still heart stopping. It is a loss that will live with me forever.

DNA DISCOVERS DEANGELO

THIS RAPIST HAD THIN LIPS, CLOSE-SET EYES, THIN LEGS (which were not muscular at all) and some flab on his stomach. The man had a slight double chin. He wore a pair of pantyhose over his head. The woman was able to get a quick look at him through her blindfold. He seemed confident, not nervous, and walked with a bit of a shuffle. The couple said he was between 5 ft. 10 in. to 6 feet tall and in his late twenties. His name is Joseph DeAngelo, and we now know he is responsible for Attack #39 because DNA has proven it.

Before DNA linked this attack to DeAngelo, some local authorities in Contra Costa County thought this attack was a copycat because the physical description of DeAngelo did not match all the descriptions of the East Area Rapist.

The M.O. in this attack is the only thing resembling past EAR attacks. A couple woke to his flashlight, they were both tied up, and dishes were placed on the husband's back while the young female was raped. DeAngelo stole money and a ring the woman was wearing. This was the first and only attack in San Ramon, California, which was unusual for the EAR. He usually attacked a few times in one area. It was also the first attack to be linked to DNA.

There are three attacks that match Joseph DeAngelo's DNA: Attack #39, #42, and #46. The DNA from these three attacks matches the DNA found at some of the murders committed in southern California.

On December 9, 1978, DeAngelo broke into a young woman's home through her patio sliding door in Danville, California. It was the 42nd attack and Joseph DeAngelo's DNA matched this crime scene, as well.

The young woman woke to a knife at her throat and DeAngelo's body straddling hers. He told her he wanted money and food for his van. He tied her hands together but did not force her to masturbate him. He masturbated himself. And he raped her twice.

The young woman told law enforcement that the rapist seemed articulate and educated. He stood between 5 ft. 9 in. and 5 ft. 11 in. tall and weighed about 150-160 lbs. This home wasn't ransacked like the majority of the other attacks. Police also used tracking dogs at this site.

Joseph DeAngelo stood there at the end of the woman's bed with his flashlight in his right hand and his gun in his left hand at Attack #46 in Danville, California. DeAngelo ordered the woman to tie her husband, then he tied her. "Where's the money? As soon as you give *us* the money, *I'll* go back to the city," DeAngelo said to them. He used singular and plurals in the same sentence. During the attack, he called the woman by an incorrect name. The East Area Rapist made very few mistakes like this. DeAngelo smelled like women's talcum powder and his hands were soft and small. She thought he tried to act tough. He was described as between 5 ft. 5 in. to 5 ft. 9 in. tall. His build was stocky, and he wore a bulky sweater, even though it was the first part of June in 1979.

When the house was silent, the victims heard a car drive up their street and stop at their home. The car sat for a moment, a car door slammed, and the car took off. The husband, probably hoping for some relief, concluded the rapist left, but DeAngelo was in the room, or maybe he came back into the room. DeAngelo then left without a sound.

THE MYSTERIOUS
PAPERS

THE SLIPPERY RAPIST WHO ATTACKED #42 WAS ABOUT
TO BE HUNTED BY three scent-tracking dogs. Law enforcement
wanted to gather as much information as possible. After his 42nd attack,
the bloodhounds were let loose. It was Saturday, December 9, 1978, in
Danville, California when the first dog led officers to the Southern
Pacific railroad tracks right behind the woman's home. The dogs eagerly
led investigators from the crime scene to the rapist's getaway. The first
dog, a half a mile, the next dog tracked further, and finally the third
dog even further.

Three folded papers pulled from a spiral notebook lay on the railroad tracks where the last dog stopped. Two pages were folded up together, and the third laid on top of them. One page was a hand-drawn
map of what law enforcement believed to be a map of a neighborhood.
They named it the "Punishment Map." On the backside of the map
was scrawled the word, "Punishment." Although the third dog stopped
at the papers on the railroad track, they have never been connected to
the attack.

The young woman described DeAngelo as articulate and educated.

He stood 5 ft. 9 inches to 5 ft. 11 inches and weighed between 150-160 pounds and had brown hair.

The "Homework Papers" is a poorly written essay, also ripped from the notebook. The essay is about General George Custer.

"Mad is the Word" is the name of the third paper found. The writer describes how his sixth-grade teacher punished him by making him write sentences. These papers had never been associated with any of the EAR or Golden State Killer attacks officially and have been a major mystery for years.

———

Yogi preferred the graveyard shift when he worked for security guard companies. Employees with the highest seniority usually worked the day shifts in town. Yogi accepted any shift they gave him. He didn't seem to mind. He had several out-of-town assignments, many of which were on weekends.

The security companies assigned him to hospitals, banks, stores, events, but mostly construction sites. Developers hired security companies to guard their newly constructed homes, lumber, new appliances, and materials from thieving opportunists during construction. Construction workers were off work by three o'clock in the afternoon and gone on weekends. Yogi complained about one construction site requiring the guards to drive around and punch a time clock to prove they made their rounds.

I searched high and low for a piece of paper one day. Yogi told me he had some in his black bag. The bag sat on our kitchen table, zipped all the way up. I unzipped it and pulled out several disorganized papers. Nothing seemed in order. On top of the pile was a hand-drawn map. It looked odd, so I asked what it was. Yogi explained why the guards traced a map for work.

A developer gave the security company a hand-drawn copy of a site plan. It was a large neighborhood under development. The security company instructed each guard to hand off the map to the guard taking the next shift. The security company designed the process of handing off the map to deter the guards from arriving late or leaving early.

Yogi always had a problem with punctuality. He wasn't in a hurry to get to work, that's for sure. During this job, Yogi's timing aggravated the person waiting for him. Like everyone else, when your shift is over you want to go home. The weekend guards traced the map, so they didn't have to wait for anyone. This is the explanation Yogi gave me, and I didn't have any reason to doubt his story.

Because the tracking dog stopped on the tracks where the papers were, they believed they could connect it to Attack #42. Many thought the East Area Rapist drew the map of a neighborhood he intended to attack in the future. Some say it could be a coincidence that the papers were on the track where the EAR escaped. The content resembles what might be considered as written by a 5th or 6th grade student. Others believe they were a planted distraction. Investigators were not able to connect the papers to Attack #42 despite the tracking dog stopping at them. I viewed that map in my kitchen in 1978.

They found the papers a couple miles from Attack #42 in Danville. Attack #39, #42, and #46 in San Ramon and Danville are the only rape attacks connected to Joseph DeAngelo through DNA. DNA from 5 murderous attacks matched Joseph DeAngelo. They were in the southern California cities of Ventura, Goleta, Dana Point, and two in Irvine, California.

What can this mean? Well, it can mean a few different things. One thing it means is that Yogi was on a railroad track a couple of miles from a rape, Attack #42, committed by Joseph DeAngelo. It doesn't prove they were partners in crime or prove any crime at all. It shows the two were in the same area at some time. One is the East Area Rapist and the other, a copycat.

―――――

Years ago, I cleaned my closet of anything pertaining to Yogi. To my surprise, I came upon one of his handmade birthday cards to me. The strange thing about it is where I found it. It was in my family album for over forty years. The album holds photos of my mother, father, and brother. I wouldn't have put his card there.

I am convinced that Yogi put the handmade card in my family album. I included a copy in this book so you can compare his printing to the "Homework Papers" handwriting. It would be difficult to prove a person's printing to their handwriting, but I see resemblances in Yogi's birthday card and the "Homework Papers," found by Law Enforcement.

The "Homework Papers" is an essay written about General George Armstrong Custer. If you found this paper on the street, your first thought might be that a sixth grader lost their homework. Poorly written, the handwriting wasn't much better. I was surprised when Yogi handed me his notebook to read what he wrote.

"Look at this. It's something I wrote," he said.

I grabbed it and started reading. After a few lines, I asked him what it was. He told me that he remembered something he had written in school a long time ago.

"And you remember what you wrote on the paper from way back then?" I asked.

"I do."

The moment my eyes landed on the paper I couldn't help but correct the mistakes. When I pointed out the errors he said, "I wanted you to read it, not correct it." I came to a quick conclusion that he wanted accolades. I tried hard to muster up a compliment.

"Nice. Very nice." I put the notebook on the table and left the room.

I squirted the soap in the kitchen sink and filled it with warm water. I shook my head at least three times and asked myself why a twenty-six-year-old guy would rewrite a composition from elementary school. It was easier to wash the dishes than figure him out. And so I did.

Yogi lived his life in the past. It didn't matter whether it was a wonderful memory or an unpleasant one. He went over old conversations and fights he had a long time ago. He showed signs of obsessive-compulsive behavior, but I didn't recognize it then.

The homemade paper birthday card and the "Homework Papers" pushed memories through the floodgates, and they all crashed like unstoppable waves. Just another corner piece to place in the Yogi puzzle.

———

Below is a transcription of the General Custer Essay known as, "Homework Papers," including errors.

"Gen George armstrong Cuser. a man well amired, but a man hated very much by many who served him. He became a general at a very young age of 23 as this, all took place during the civil war, Custer after the war was dropped to his permanent rank of captain, ae he fought more, he made more enemies, especially fighting against the indians in the southwest. In 1876 the government planned to Round up the Suix and Cheynre and put te on reservations. Custer's regiment joined the expedition, commanded by general alfred H. Terry. as Terry's scout's neported indican villages throughout the mountain territory, Terry ordered Custer to find... (crossed out). Then as custer searched for the villages, custer and his men found a vally that ran allong the little big horn river. Custer expecting only around 1000, had not ~~expected~~ realzing there word be around 5000 indians would (above would is the word *THAT*) fight back. It was the largest gathering of 'hostile' tribes in the mountain territory. The battle (crossed out) would

be one of the deadlest and most strangest battles between the indians and the white man. 225 union men,
including Custer, died that day by couragous but hostile
indians that would do anything to save their homes and
there families."

Yogi had a sixth-grade teacher who he idolized. He taught math but
spent a lot of time talking about history during class. His teacher was
a history buff who told stories that intrigued Yogi enough to make him
want to become one too. Yogi was a class clown, disruptive, and talked
too much. Yogi's teacher wouldn't put up with it and punished him by
making him write sentences, lose his field trip privileges, or miss recess.
It was a love-hate relationship in Yogi's mind. I didn't see this paper but
heard the stories.

"Mad Is The Word" is an essay describing how terrible the teacher
made his life by making him write sentences as punishment for his
behavior.

"Mad Is The Word," including errors:

"Mad is the word, the word that reminds me of 6th grade. I hated
that year...I wish I had know what was going to be going on during
my 6th grade year, the last and worst year of elementary school. Mad
is the word that remains in my head about my dreadful year as a 6th
grader. My madness was one that caused disapointments that hurt
me very much. Dissapointments from my teacher, such as feild trips
that were planed, then canncled. My 6th grade teacher gave me a lot of
dissapointments which made me very mad and made me built a state
of hatred in my heart, no one ever let me down that hard before and
I never hated anyone as much as I did him. Disapointment wasn't the
only reason that made me mad in my sixth grade class, another was
getting in trouble at school espeically talking thats what really bugged

me was writing sentances, those awful sentance that my teacher made…
me write, hours and hours Id sit and write 50-100-150 sentance day and
night I write those dreadful Paragraphs which embarrased me and more
inportant it made me ashamed of myself which in turn, deep down in
side made me realize that writing sentance wasn't fair it wasn't fair to
make me suffer like that, it just wasn't fair to make me suffer like that,
it just wasn't fair to make me sit and wright until my bones aked, until
my hand felt every horrid pain it ever had and as I wrote, I got mader
and mader until I cried, I cried because I was ashamed I cried because
I was discusted, I cried because I was mad, and I cried for myself, kid
who kept on having to write those dane sentances. My Angryness from
Sixth grade will scar my memory for life and I will be ashamed for my
sixth grade year forever."

———

In December 1977, a person who claimed to be the East Area Rapist
sent this typed written poem, "Excitement's Crave" to the Sacramento
Bee Newspaper, KVIE television station, and the Sacramento may-
or's office. I have never seen or read this poem during my time with
Yogi.

"Excitement's Crave," (including errors):
All those mortal's surviving birth
Upon facing maturity,
Take inventory of their worth
To prevailing society.
Choosing values becomes a task;
Oneself must seek satisfaction.
The selected route will unmask
Character when plans take action.
Accepting some work to perform

At fixed pay, but promise for more,
Is a recognized social norm,
As is decorum, seeking lore.
Achieving while others lifting
Should be cause for deserving fame.
Leisure tempts excitement seeking,
What's right and expected seems tame.
"Jessie James" has been seen by all,
And "Son of Sam" has an author.
Others now feel temptations call.
Sacramento should make an offer.
To make a movie of my life
That will pay for my planned exile.
Just now I'd like to add the wife
of a Mafia lord to my file.
Your East Area Rapist
And deserving pest.
See you in the press or on T.V.

A GOOD DROP

A THIRTEEN-YEAR-OLD CHILD WOKE TO A STRANGER'S HAND OVER her mouth. His body lay on top of hers. It was the summer of 1979, and she became the 47th person attacked by the East Area Rapist, and the youngest one. The tip of his knife on her skin caused her to obey his every command.

The perpetrator gagged and tied her hands and feet before continuing his assault. He lubricated his penis and made her massage it with her hands behind her back, just like all the other times he violated unsuspecting sleeping women. Only this was a child.

"Have you ever fucked before? Gimme a good drop or I'll kill you." He raped the young girl and left soon after.

Law enforcement brought a tracking dog to the scene, which led them to the same spot where the perpetrator of Attack #45 was assumed to be. The dog remembered the same scent.

The child described the rapist as broad shouldered, in his late twenties, and about 6 feet tall. She told police he used a fake Spanish accent. He stayed in her home for about twenty minutes. That horrible twenty minutes will last her lifetime.

"WHAT'S GOING ON IN THAT FUNNY LITTLE MIND OF

YOURS?" I asked Yogi. His blue eyes had a faraway look as he got ready for work. Tiny clicks shot out from his mouth. I dangled his t-shirt in front of his face. He sat up quickly and snatched it out of my hand. He seemed startled that I had interrupted his train of thought.

"Jeez, what's up with you?" But he still hadn't answered my question.

He turned and looked up at me. "I'm just thinking about driving the cab tonight," he said. "That fucking dispatcher better give me a good drop. Every night it's the same drivers that get the good drops. He plays favorites. I just know he's getting kickbacks from them."

"Well, ignore all that and find your own fares."

"It doesn't work like that, Helen. Maybe if I'm parked in front of the bus depot or the airport, but the dispatcher keeps putting me in residential areas. People aren't walking around looking for cab rides there. They call the cab company for a ride. I'll be picking up little old ladies at the grocery store and dropping them off a mile away. The other bastards will get the good drops."

"Gimme a good drop." This phrase has been a mystery to detectives for years. Most believed it referenced ejaculation or had something to do with sex. The East Area Rapist only used this phrase during this particular attack. The first time I read that sentence online, I knew exactly what it meant. Only a small group of people used the term.

In the 1970s, they equipped cabs with meters. When a person got into the cab for a ride, the first thing a cab driver would do before moving was "drop the flag down." The cost of the cab ride began at that point with a surcharge. The meter kept track of miles driven and the charge for the ride.

Cab drivers had "pickups" and "drops." A pickup was where the cab driver picked up the person. The end of the ride was the drop.

Drivers would envy the cabbies who got fares to or from the airport. In the 70s, most homes were 30 miles away from the Sacramento Metropolitan Airport. A 30-mile ride from the airport to someone's home meant a longer ride, which meant more money and usually a bigger tip. It was "a good drop."

The dispatcher chose drivers to work a certain area during their shift and rotated days or weeks. This is how Yogi learned the streets of Sacramento so well. He was familiar with each area, all the shortcuts and all the long ways around.

Our daily existence depended on Yogi's tips from cab driving. While moaning and terrified victims waited for the rapist's next move, the East Area Rapist stuffed his face with leftovers and before leaving, stole their change. Two important reasons Yogi needed to bring home change were to provide food for both of us to eat the next day and provide the illusion that he worked all night.

A couple of drivers might share the same car for their shifts. It wasn't unusual for drivers to leave a bag in the trunk with snacks, writing paper, or books. It was long before the internet, so drivers relied on other things to keep them occupied until they were assigned a pick-up. Most drivers kept a gym bag with these types of items in it. Sometimes Yogi brought his bag home and sometimes he would leave it in the cab's trunk. Checking the bag never crossed my mind. I trusted Yogi and wasn't very curious.

What better job could you have if you were a rapist than to be a night shift cab driver? Picture yourself working as a cab driver in the middle of the night. The night dispatcher has no idea where you are; except where you tell him. There weren't cell phones, so the communication was through a two-way radio. An all-night shift, when most people slept, meant few witnesses. It wouldn't raise suspicions if a cab was parked near a business or home.

Driving slowly through a neighborhood to scope out something might look like a lost cab driver searching for an address.

It would be easy to screen each cab ride, looking for a potential victim or learn valuable information from them to use later when they forget all about you. Phone numbers of your fares were easy to get from the dispatcher.

Most cab drivers try to engage in simple conversations with their fares. The cab driver is doing more than just driving you to your destination. He is providing a pleasant drive and engaging in small talk to increase his tips. It's not only a driving job, it's also a sales position. It is the driver's way of making daily income to supplement his paycheck.

He might ask questions about your children, their ages, and your pets. People love to talk about themselves, their families, and their vacation plans to cab drivers. Fares aren't afraid to unload personal information. They don't think they will see the driver again.

If you helped your fares with their luggage or groceries into their house, you could learn the layout of their home. A person's bathroom can provide personal information from their medicine cabinet.

The 70s were a different time than now. Most people had their phone numbers listed in city phone books. Cab drivers, delivery drivers, and others hoping to find addresses used the Polk's Directory.

Homes didn't use cameras or surveillance video. Many people slept with their windows open on warm summer nights. In some neighborhoods, many didn't lock their doors.

It was a time when most people had a picture in their mind of what a rapist looked like and how he acted. If a person was kind, helpful, and a humorous cab driver, there would be no reason to suspect that person to be anything other than just that. Yogi's forte was making people feel comfortable around him. Like Mr. Clarke.

"Gimme a good drop." It is my guess Yogi accidentally said those words aloud before he sexually assaulted the thirteen-year-old child.

DUMBFOUNDED

HE DONNED A MASK FOR THE LAST TIME IN NORTHERN CALIFORNIA. On July 5, 1979, Attack #48 was in the East Area Rapist's sights. At 4:30 a.m., a husband woke to a vision of the EAR standing by his bedroom door. He was putting his mask over his head. The husband told police the intruder had a thick neck. The rapist wore a dark blue jacket with what looked like CORN or Coors written in white on the left breast of the jacket or CCC. This windbreaker matches the description in Attack #45 in Walnut Creek. The husband was about 6 ft. 2 inches and weighed 220 pounds.

"Who the fuck do you think you are? What the fuck are you doing here?" While he kept screaming at the intruder, the wife ran downstairs to escape. The EAR stood and stared at the husband as if he was in shock and wasn't sure how to respond. He was dumbfounded. Their neighbor heard the wife screaming and called the police.

The husband was put under hypnosis for a thorough description of the perpetrator. He described the stranger to be about 5 ft 10 inches to 6 feet, in his mid-twenties, and thin with athletic shoulders. His eyes were light colored and sleepy looking. The eyelashes were full and long.

Yogi's neck was thick. Was the blue windbreaker folded in such a way that it covered up some letters? Under pressure, with adrenaline screeching through the victim, could he have missed some letters?

I split most of my free time between Mary and Betty. Betty's mother worked in real estate and had many job contacts. She helped Betty get an apartment manager's job in Carmichael, California. The apartment building had 22 garden apartments. Betty thrived in this position. She handled all the move-ins and move-outs and dealt with all the renters. It was an onsite position, so a two-bedroom apartment and free utilities were part of her monthly income. She gave Yogi a lightweight blue windbreaker when we lived on 38th Street. She told him it didn't fit her, and he could have it. On the left-hand side of the jacket in white lettering was, "Custom Carpet Care." Custom Carpet Care was a carpet cleaning company Betty used at the Sutter Gardens Apartments. I'm not sure if the company gave it to her as a marketing piece or if an employee of CCC left it in an apartment after a job.

The intruder's reaction to the husband resembles Yogi's demeanor when you do the unexpected. If Yogi expected any confrontation, he practiced exactly what he would say. For work, he was ready to get out of trouble. With me, he could lie quickly without hemming and hawing. Always ready for any scenario.

Yogi and I didn't argue very often. I was calm, unless I saw someone being used or abused. Then I could come undone. It was easier to stick up for someone else before I stuck up for myself, except one day. We lived on P Street. Yogi stood there drinking his coffee. I sat quietly in the old blue chair. That morning, Yogi blew up about something. His face was red with anger, he threw his hot cup of coffee at the dining room wall, then looked at me with a "What are you going to do about it?" look. Coffee spewed around the room and onto the wall as the cup broke into several pieces. The wall stared at us with brown liquid dripping down to the floor. I rose and met his face with mine, body stiff, throat growling, teeth clenched, and ordered Yogi, "Now go clean up the mess you just made. That was my favorite cup."

He froze in what looked like fear. His eyes were staring at me with no reply. Yogi did not expect my reaction. Dumbfounded, he tried to process what happened. He didn't know what to do next, so he stood there staring. My reaction didn't fit into the play he orchestrated in his mind.

Attack #48 was the last attack by the East Area Rapist in northern California. The EAR must have thought the husband saw his face and could identify him. Law Enforcement surmised that a life event might have taken place in the EAR's life to suddenly halt the rapes. I became pregnant with our son, Benjamin, in May 1979 and found out in July. He was born at the end of January 1980.

Law enforcement claims the EAR moved to Southern California and first struck in Santa Barbara County in October 1979. The rapes were more savage than the northern California crimes, and with a different MO. After violently raping these victims, the perpetrator tortured them and either shot them or slaughtered them to death.

COPYCAT?

HIS NICKNAME DESCRIBES BEST HOW HE COMMITTED HIS CRIMES. The Bedroom Basher was a serial rapist and murderer who committed his crimes between 1978-1979. He broke into single women's homes while they slept. He bludgeoned the female with a board, raped her, then bludgeoned her to death. Some of his victims lived through the horrible crime. His sixth victim, Dianna Green, was pregnant and lived, but her unborn child did not survive. The beating left Dianna unable to communicate. The jury found her husband, Kevin Lee Green, guilty in October 1980. He spent sixteen years in prison for the crime he did not commit. After years in prison, they exonerated him through DNA.

In 1996, Law Enforcement arrested Gerald Parker for the Bedroom Basher crimes, and he is currently on death row at San Quentin State Prison in California. He was in and out of prison for various violent crimes over the years. He violated parole and had to give a blood sample. Through a DNA match, they caught him.

The times that the Bedroom Basher raped and bludgeoned women coincided with the time Joseph DeAngelo began his spree of violent rapes that ended in murder. The Bedroom Basher committed his crimes in Orange County. Many believe DeAngelo imitated the Bedroom

Basher to throw off law enforcement. He was on a murdering spree in the same vicinity, at about the same time.

DeAngelo's penchant for murder began when he shot Professor Claude Snelling in Visalia in 1975. He also shot to kill Officer McGowan in December 1975. The East Area Rapist's reign of terror began in 1976. Despite the women who fought back or made it difficult to rape them, the East Area Rapist did not maim or kill his 48 victims in Northern California.

Through DNA, law enforcement linked DeAngelo to murders in Goleta, Dana Point, Irvine, and Ventura. DeAngelo raped, then bludgeoned these victims to death without mercy.

Some believe Joseph DeAngelo was a copycat who used his employment as a police officer to his benefit. He was privy to the sordid details of crimes and could carry them out without bringing attention to himself. DeAngelo killed in Visalia and in Southern California, yet not in Northern California. Did he copy a non-killing East Area Rapist? Did he then move to Southern California and copy a bludgeoning killer known as The Bedroom Basher?

Others believe Joseph DeAngelo is a serial rapist who *graduated* to serial murder. Although not all serial rapists end up murdering their victims, there have been known cases. In DeAngelo's case there could have been triggering thoughts or enraging events driving him to more aggression. Location, timing, and personal events may have been a factor. We may never know.

Copycat or not, the end result is heartbreaking.

MOM KNOWS A
VOYEUR

BETTY HAD A HAND IN SHAPING MY CAREER IN REAL ESTATE. The property management company promoted her to manage a larger apartment building. She gave her supervisor a gleaming referral of Yogi and me. Free rent, free utilities, and a small salary turned our lives around and it felt good.

After we moved into our new place, we flew to Massachusetts to get married. Shirley arranged the wedding and reception for us. We met many of her dear friends and family. We planned to meet Yogi's natural father in Rhode Island, but a heavy storm kept us from flying that evening.

When we returned to California, it was time to begin managing the apartments. Next to about every front door were boxes, old barbecues, bikes, torn up summer chairs, and miscellaneous junk. Our supervisor, Mary, dropped by and told me there was no time like the present to meet every resident and let them know they all needed to remove everything from their porches. I was about to send Mary back to where she came from. The thought scared the crap out of me, but Mary walked to each apartment with me, and I realized one of my gifts was relating to people from all walks of life. It was the little push and huge amount of confidence Mary had in me that helped me take the first giant step that day. Mary was pivotal in my success not only that day, but the days ahead. She boosted my confidence in everything, and I will always be grateful for her friendship.

Six months later, Yogi's birth mother flew to California for Benjamin's first birthday. We enjoyed the entire week visiting with her. She filled the void I had deep within me for a loving mother. I cherished having her in my world and was happy to see her again. One night, when it was time to go to bed, Yogi said, "Goodnight," as he headed for the front door. Shirley had a puzzled and disappointed look on her face. She looked Yogi in the eyes and calmly said, "Oh, you're still doing that, huh?" Oh dear, I was sure I knew what she meant. I'm sure his adopted mother shared the story about Yogi's arrest for peeping into windows and burglarizing homes and whatever else he did. I invented a reason to leave the room and as I did, I heard the front door shut. Yogi left even though his mother's reaction implied that he should not go. I'm sure they exchanged words I was never privy to. Maybe she knew more than I should have known. Yogi acted naïve about the situation when I brought it up after she left. The saddest part is that was the last time we had any contact with her. We never saw her or heard from her again. In fact, it was also the last time we interacted with Yogi's adopted family. Benjamin never experienced how loving and wonderful his natural grandmother could be.

The apartment was sold to another investor, so we moved on to manage another property on Annadale Lane. My salary increased, but the living standards left much to be desired. After cleaning up the complex from undesirables, non-payers, and a pedophile, I was offered a new position right next door. I didn't hesitate to hop onto that opportunity. We moved into a large 2-bedroom apartment with a dishwasher and large backyard. Life was grand! Or so it seemed.

23 CENTS

THAT MORNING IN 1985 WHEN I POINTED YOGI'S .38 SNUB-NOSE REVOLVER at his head while he was still in bed was the day reality knocked at my front door. I tiptoed into our bedroom, overcome with grief for what I had learned, but filled with unspeakable bravery.

He rolled over so fast to see if I had his gun on him, and it startled me. The coward was fake sleeping. I continued to act like Clint Eastwood in one of his cop movies, only I had real hate in my eyes.

As I stared Yogi down, I wanted to detect some kind of fear in his eyes, or a palpitating heart and uncontrollable trembling. Not a quiver, nor a shake. He lay there calm, not making the slightest move, and lies dripped from his mouth for the next twenty minutes. As he spoke, visions of bits and pieces of him splattered on my bedroom wall floated through my thoughts like a dream.

He tried to tell me she was just a lying 14-year-old girl trying to get him in trouble for letting her have a beer. I saw through him, and he realized I wasn't buying what he was saying. The revolver stayed put as he searched for another excuse.

"She came into the living room with a light blanket wrapped around her. She stood in front of the T.V. light and stretched both arms out, holding on to the blanket behind her as she faced the T.V., then laid down on the floor. I saw her silhouette through the blanket. She did that on purpose to tantalize me."

Like a bag of tricks, Yogi carried a bag of excuses for every horrendous thing he did, from molesting this girl to peering at his sister, raping the girl in Boston, and raping countless Japanese women when he was in the military stationed in Japan. And who knows how many others? The teen girl from down the street was another addition to Yogi's endless list of victims for which he did not get caught.

The police never showed up. I imagine he had a set story for them if they came calling. Yogi could muster up believable lies in sometimes what seemed like seconds. Sadly, no mother, brother, uncle, or friend of the teen called to turn him in. And sadly, neither did I. I tried to make myself believe that if it were true, someone would have shown up. Many years later, I learned victims don't always tell.

My million-dollar feeling from the night before shrunk to about 23 cents. My body filled in for his fantasy of being with the young girl on my living room floor. Nothing more. I met him for the first time. Yogi was nothing more than a serial rapist, a molester, and a pedophile. I laid the gun on the dresser, grabbed my purse, and left. My sweet son's love for his daddy is the only reason I didn't pull the trigger that day. After knowing what I know now, I wish I had.

———

No one knew my forty-five-year-old secret about Yogi attacking women in Japan, and no one could ever know that horrific truth. Not even my "no matter what" friend, Mary. I could tell Mary anything, no matter what, and we would still be friends. But I just couldn't tell her about that night with the teen or what Yogi did in Japan.

Had the horrible truth about Yogi gotten out, it would have ruined one little boy's perception of his perfect, loving daddy forever. It would have kept his father from changing into a good person, (which never happened). I would have had to deal with the reality of who he was and explain why I was still with him. Shame would have followed all of us. So, I buried that secret of the young girl way down deep, and never spoke of that night or the other horrible secrets Yogi told me when we first met. It was a cabbagehead move to stay with Yogi after learning what he did in Japan. I was young, desperate, alone, and insecure - running away from my childhood and running into someone I thought loved me and would be with me the rest of my life.

After that night, I stayed with Mary for a few days, then returned home. It wasn't easy to do, but Benjamin and my management position at work drew me back. In retrospect I know if I were truthful about what happened, my friends would have helped me. My biggest hurdle was keeping Benjamin safe from the knowledge of his father. With that information, I trusted no one.

A promotion to another property twenty minutes away came at a perfect time. Mornings were unbearable, sitting in the kitchen sipping my coffee, staring at the spot where my husband lay next to his prey. I envisioned him smoking a cigarette and drinking a Coors beer while he plotted his moves on how he would devour the young girl on our floor. Much worse, I had to watch my six-year-old son sitting in front of the T.V. playing with his G.I. Joes, as I mulled over in my mind what happened in that very spot. My angel faced little one could never learn what a vile father he had. I swore to myself I would never share Yogi's secrets with anyone. Benjamin discovering the truth about his father was a chance I wasn't willing to take.

I'm sure I reeked of humiliation. It became hard to face my friends. Yogi continued his typical routine with no sign of shame. I'm positive he reassured himself she was to blame, and he moved on. His value system remained broken, like a toy that doesn't work. You continue to put good batteries in it, and it still doesn't run right.

I accepted the promotion to manage the apartments on Tallyho

Drive. The property was in Sacramento, close to Rancho Cordova. Seventy-four apartments sprawled out over a large parcel of land. The nicest people lived there. I looked forward to working at the apartments and it became my favorite place to live.

———

Yogi had a new neighborhood to roam. As always, he left late in the evening for his solo walk. Many years have passed since the East Area Rapist attacks. Now I wonder what crimes happened on those solo walks in every neighborhood we lived in.

The M.O. likely changed, but in hindsight, as I piece together this ugly puzzle, I believe the rapes and voyeurism did not. He grew older, heavier, and became less agile. A quick escape would not be easy for him. But a gun or knife has a way of granting power to anyone using it, no matter what shape they're in. Perhaps there were fewer rapes, or the target area and M.O. changed.

Yogi didn't change and he didn't see the light. I am sure he was involved in the East Area rapes. In 2016, the FBI shined their lights on the forty-year-old crimes. Information tucked away for years was finally shared with the public. We were all encouraged to mentally re-visit the 70s to see if we remembered anyone resembling the rapist who still remained at large. Before 2016, the thought of Yogi sharing any involvement with these crimes never entered my mind.

Between 2016 and 2018, I called and emailed every law enforcement agency to tell my story. I was never given the opportunity. In 2018, Joseph DeAngelo was arrested at his home. I strained to make myself believe Yogi was innocent. I worked hard to un-see the composite that stared back at me. Thoughts of Yogi woke me from my sleep and a small fire burned in the pit of my stomach. Joseph DeAngelo was not the only one. I had no choice but to write *Cabbagehead*. I knew they both shared my nickname for him, the King of Creeps.

Nothing was ever the same between us after the molestation on my living room floor. Even moving to a new place didn't erase the wretched memories of Yogi's past. I tried to forget, but the memory stayed on my mind. It was everywhere. I saw it in brown-haired young girls, thin white blankets, green shirts, wrapping myself in a towel every morning after my shower, and I saw it forever in Yogi's eyes. The most beautiful sparkling blue eyes looked black and evil to me. It was as if every girl he raped looked out of those eyes to show me how much darkness was inside him. Then I realized I didn't have to endure it. I didn't have to survive anything anymore. I could just leave the horror story, just as I left the last one at the private school. And life would be good.

It wasn't easy for me. It would still take some years to build up my confidence before leaving him, but eventually I did. Our relationship died. We were roommates with one common bond: the love for Benjamin. As time passed, Yogi morphed into a stranger. It was easy to stay because Yogi worked the graveyard shift and I worked days. We briefly passed one another each day and hadn't slept together in years. My weekends were spent with Benjamin and close friends.

My friends became more important than anything in my life, besides Benjamin. They became my family. A family that showed up when times were fantastic and when times weren't so great. A family who encouraged me, shot down my self-doubt, and just plain loved me the way I was. It was Carla, Mary, Lily, and even a new friend that unknowingly gave me courage and pushed me forward to make the changes I wanted and needed.

And Yogi? He imprisoned himself with his thoughts and lies. His own mind tortured him every morning when he woke up to face another day. Just like the sin eaters he told me about, he tried to eat his sins away, becoming morbidly obese in the process. Yogi returned to self-medicating with street drugs to hide his guilt and cloud his thoughts so he wouldn't have to admit to himself that he was a monster. He was a heavy drinker, addicted to crank (methamphetamine), and as his death certificate indicated, he was morbidly obese. All of it took a toll on his body. On April 8, 2011, he died of a heart attack in a small apartment in downtown Sacramento. He was 59 years old. And, really, nobody cared. I was surprised to get a call from the county announcing his death. After all, it had been over twenty years since we were together. No next-of-kin could be found.

Some may ask, "So what does it matter, anyway? Joseph DeAngelo murdered and raped people. They have DNA for rape attacks #39, #42, and #46. They have some DNA for some murders in southern California. He admitted to all the crimes. He is guilty. He deserves the eleven life sentences he received and then some. All the rapes have far passed the statute of limitations." I agree Joseph DeAngelo is guilty of horrendous crimes and deserves much more than his sentences.

So, what does it matter? Truth will always matter. It never gets old, and it doesn't have a statute of limitations. Because next time there is a crime and it is obvious there is more than one criminal, they both should have to pay for their own crimes.

Law Enforcement passed judgment on one man, despite the glaring information that there was more than one rapist. They closed their eyes and ears and that allowed them to close the case. Maybe they thought the case was so old, they wanted to bring closure for all the victims. I understand that. But don't the victims and public deserve the complete truth?

It was important for me to tell you, and it is important for you to know. Imagine if Yogi were alive today, now that DeAngelo (in 2020) took the rap for all the rapes and murders. He'd have his feet up on the coffee table, sipping his cold beer, and knowing he was safe from any knocks on the door. I am reminded of what he said to Mary and me when the subject of the East Area rapist came up: *"He must be good if they haven't caught him yet."*

We are all lucky to be free from both monsters.

Not everything is as it seems,
and not everything that seems is.
~Jose de Sousa Saramago

PSYCHOLOGICAL PROFILE OF THE EAR

Below is a psychological profile of the East Area Rapist/Original Night Stalker. It was compiled by Leslie D'Ambrosia, a professional criminal profiler. I have compared the profile to Yogi.

White male–
Yes

Dressed well and would not stand out in upscale neighborhoods–
Yogi dressed normally for his age and for the 1970s. I'm not sure he wouldn't stand out in an upscale neighborhood.

Drove a well-maintained car–
No

Emotional age of 26 to 30 at the time the crimes were committed–
This is true.

Engaged in deviant paraphilic behavior and brutal sex in his personal life–
I'm not a doctor, but knowing Yogi's history, I can without a doubt agree with the statement. The police arrested him when he was fifteen for voyeurism and burglary. He was a rapist in the Marine Corps. He engaged in fantasy sex. I did not experience brutal sex with him.

Knowledgeable about police investigations–
Yogi was a military policeman in the Marine Corps.

Had some means of income, but did not work early hours–
Yogi worked as a cab driver from 6 p.m. to 6 a.m. These work hours and the flexibility of the job gave Yogi the perfect cover and opportunity.

Intelligent and articulate–
He was of normal intelligence and articulate. He was a history buff.

Neat and well organized–
Yes. I would almost consider Yogi OCD. He liked to do the laundry and dishes because he wanted everything organized a certain way.

Self-assured and confident in his abilities–
Yes

Capable of ejaculating with both consenting and non-consenting partners–
Yogi was capable of ejaculating with me. I am uncertain of his non-consenting partners.

Was a skilled cat burglar and may have begun that way–
Yogi started at the age of fifteen and a half.

Was in good physical condition–
Yogi was in excellent physical condition.

Would appear harmless–
Yogi appeared harmless. He had the gift of conversation. He was friendly and had a way of putting you at ease through laughter.

Would be described as arrogant, domineering, chronic liar–
I would not describe Yogi as arrogant or domineering. He was a chronic liar. He did not get along with any superiors in the workplace. I think that is the reason he lasted longer in positions where his supervisor was not present, i.e., cab driving, security, and convenience store cashier.

Did not enter long-term relationships-
We were together for fifteen years, but I believe only because of my naiveté and fear of being alone.

Slept with prostitutes-
Yes, before we met and more than likely after we met.

Would continue committing violent crimes until imprisoned or dead-
Well, I'm not sure.

Had a submissive wife who tolerated his behavior-
I don't consider myself submissive. I was naïve to Yogi's behavior. He wasn't arrogant or domineering at all.

Started out as a voyeur-
Yes

Hated women for real or perceived wrongs-
He hated his mother and sister. To rape so many women in Japan, he would have to be a woman- hater.

Would be described by those who knew him as manipulative and a chronic liar-
Those two words describe Yogi perfectly. He was a con artist and a master manipulator.

MORE THAN ONE
PHYSICAL DESCRIPTION

The descriptions below were given to law enforcement by the victims after their attacks. It's interesting to see just how the EAR descriptions vary when they stand alone.

About Hair:

Attack #1. A lot of dark leg and arm hair

Attack #3. Dark pubic hair

Attack #4. Dark pubic hair

Attack #5. Thick, dark head hair

Attack #7. Heavy dark-colored leg and arm hair

Attack #9. Brown head and leg hair

Attack #13. Legs were white and hairy.

Attack #16. Abrasive leg hair, as if shaved. Hairy backside.

Attack #17. Dark blonde collar-length hair

Attack #20. Dark brown collar-length hair. Very hairy legs.

Attack #21. Very hairy legs

Attack #26. Light-colored hair

Attack #35. Hairy backside, big hairy thighs

Attack #40. Dark haired

Attack #42. Brown hair, hairy legs

Attack #44. Brown leg hair

Attack #46. DNA/ Soft light-brown hair

Judging by the photos of Joseph DeAngelo online, I would describe his hair color as light brown to blonde. It was straight. Usually, a person with lighter hair and skin color does not have hairy limbs or backsides.

Yogi's hair color was a darker brown. His arms, legs and backside were hairy. His thigh hair was like stubble, as if he shaved it. He never admitted to that. The hair on his head was wavy. The longer it grew, the curlier it looked.

About Physical Build:
Attack #1. Muscular legs, broad shouldered, muscular build
Attack #2. Muscular frame
Attack #3. Muscular frame, muscular legs, military bearing
Attack #4. Muscular, but lean legs
Attack #5. Medium weight
Attack #10. Regular build
Attack #11. Medium build
Attack #16. Medium build, muscular thighs, no pot belly
Attack #18. Slender build
Attack #19. Slender build
Attack #20. Stocky build
Attack #22 Slender build
Attack #23. Slender build
Attack #25. Muscular, fit.
Attack #27. Thin to medium build
Attack #28. Thin to medium build
Attack #29. Thin to medium build
Attack #32. Medium build, fit, no fat.
Attack #34. Slender build
Attack #35. Medium build, big thighs
Attack #39. DNA/ Thin legs, not muscular, a little flab on stomach
Attack #43. Medium build, no fat
Attack #45. No fat

Attack #46. DNA/ Stocky build

Attack #47. Not heavy, broad shoulders

Attack #48. Thin build, "athletic shoulders"

About Penis Size:

Attack #1. Not well endowed

Attack #3. Seemed fairly small

Attack #5. Felt small

Attack #7. Small penis

Attack #11. 5-6 inches

Attack #12. 4-5 inches and skinny

Attack #13. Extremely small

Attack #16. 5 inches, thin

Attack #17. 5 inches, diameter of a quarter

Attack #18. Very small

Attack #19. 5 inches

Attack #21. 5 inches

Attack #22. Short

Attack #25. Fairly large around with a small head

Attack #26. Large around, short

Attack #27. 5 inches

Attack #29. Small penis

Attack #30. Small, maybe 3 inches

Attack #31. Not very large

Attack #33. Small

Attack #34. Small

Attack #35. Long, thin

Attack #36. 3-4 inches, not erect

Attack #38. 3 inches erect

Attack #40. Small

Attack #41. 5-6 inches

Attack #44. 3 inches

Age Approximations:

Attack #1. Early 20's

Attack #3. 18-20

Attack #5. 30's

Attack #6. About 25

Attack #9. 18-23

Attack #12. 30's

Attack #13. Early 20's

Attack #15. 20's

Attack #16. Mid-20's

Attack #19. 25-35

Attack #24. 20's to early 30's

Attack #25. 20's

Attack #28. Early 20's

Attack #30. Mid 20's#2. Under 20

Attack #31. 20's to early 30's

Attack #32. Mid 20's

Attack #34. Early 20's

Attack #39. Late 20's

Attack #41. 20's

Attack #44. Late 20's to early 30's

Attack#46. 20's

Attack #47. Late 20's

Attack #48. Mid 20's

SOURCES

1   *Hunting A Psychopath* by Richard Shelby
2   *Sudden Terror* by Larry Crompton
3   *I'll Be Gone in the Dark* by Michelle McNamara
4   GoldenStateKiller.com, Website information from JJMcR's site and EARONS Composite
5   EAR/ONS/GSK Pro boards, Reddit online
6   unresolved.me, a Podcast by Michael Whelan
7   Casefile: True Crime Podcast by Anonymous Host
8   12-26-75.com The Physical Description of the VR, Podcast.
9   "Exclusive: East Area Rapist Survivor Speaks," October 18, 2018, a YouTube Video

Made in the USA
Middletown, DE
03 July 2022

68364728R00139